Ray Argyle

Ray Argyle has worked in journalism and public relations and is the author of three biographies, a history of Canadian political campaigns, and a novel set in Victorian Canada.

He has served as a member of the Board of Trustees of The McMichael Canadian Art Collection, Kleinburg, Ontario, and the Scarborough (Toronto) Board of Education. He is secretary-treasurer of the Foundation for the Advancement of Canadian Letters (FACL) and is the only Canadian to have been elected a Fellow of the   sociation.

Ray has contribu   including The *National Post*, Ca   *ver*), and *Reader's Digest*. His v   e lives in Kingston, Ontario.

D1472975

A QUEST BIOGRAPHY

JOEY SMALLWOOD

SCHEMER AND DREAMER

RAY ARGYLE

DUNDURN
TORONTO

Editor: Matt Baker
Design: Courtney Horner
Printer: Webcom

Library and Archives Canada Cataloguing in Publication

Argyle, Ray
    Joey Smallwood : schemer and dreamer / Ray Argyle.

Includes bibliographical references and index.
Issued also in electronic formats.
ISBN 978-1-4597-0369-8

    1. Smallwood, Joseph R., 1900-1991. 2. Prime ministers--
Newfoundland and Labrador--Biography. 3. Newfoundland
and Labrador--Politics and government--20th century.
I. Title.

FC2175.1.S63A75 2012   971.8'04092   C2012-900118-X

1   2   3   4   5   16   15   14   13   12

We acknowledge the support of the Canada Council for the Arts and the Ontario Arts Council for our publishing program. We also acknowledge the financial support of the Government of Canada through the Canada Book Fund and Livres Canada Books, and the Government of Ontario through the Ontario Book Publishing Tax Credit and the Ontario Media Development Corporation.

Printed and bound in Canada.
www.dundurn.com

Visit us at
Dundurn.com
Definingcanada.ca
@dundurnpress
Facebook.com/dundurnpress

Dundurn	Gazelle Book Services Limited	Dundurn
3 Church Street, Suite 500	White Cross Mills	2250 Military Road
Toronto, Ontario, Canada	High Town, Lancaster, England	Tonawanda, NY
M5E 1M2	LA1 4XS	U.S.A. 14150

Never say die! Never give in! Turn a deaf ear to the timid and faithless.
And then at last, if the very fates do defeat us, go down, not with a whimper, but defiantly to the end!
— Joseph R. Smallwood, *I Chose Canada*

Contents

Acknowledgements

The opportunity to re-examine the life of a man as fascinating and complex as Joey Smallwood comes to only the most fortunate of biographers.

I am grateful to Michael Carroll and Kirk Howard at Dundurn for having entrusted me with this task and to my editor, Matt Baker, for his meticulous care and attention.

In writing this fresh appreciation of the man most remembered for having brought Newfoundland and Labrador into Canada, my aim has been to provide a modern perspective on the life of Joseph R. Smallwood, and to coax out the human side of the man. I have drawn on archival documents, journals, books, and newspaper accounts covering various aspects of his life and times. His early biographers, most notably Richard Gwyn and Harold Horwood, laid out the essentials facts, as did Joey Smallwood himself in his memoir, *I Chose Canada*. All of these sources have been helpful in understanding the aspirations and fears that motivated the man whose influence on his province extended over half a century.

I also had the assistance of people who knew Joey Smallwood, worked with him, mourned him, and who have recorded the consequences of his policies and acts on the lives of his fellow Newfoundlanders and Labradorians. They include the Honourable Clyde Wells, who served in the Smallwood Cabinet and later became premier and then chief justice of the Supreme Court of Newfoundland and Labrador, and the Honourable Edward Roberts, a former lieutenant governor, Smallwood Cabinet minister, and leader of the Liberal Party. The staff of the Centre for Newfoundland Studies at Memorial University helped me scour through the files of the J.R. Smallwood Collections. Political journalists David Bartlett and James McLeod gave me helpful advice. Dale Russell FitzPatrick and Joseph Smallwood, grandchildren of Joey Smallwood, shared their recollections of him. Others too numerous to mention contributed nuggets of knowledge invaluable to a "come from away" in search of insights into the life of their province's most celebrated figure.

Introduction

A Land Like No Other

> Who out of the fogs of time past first sailed our way?
> What breed of European first set foot on these eastern
> shores of North America?
>> — Kevin Major, *As Near to Heaven by Sea:*
>> *A History of Newfoundland*

Morning mists envelop the sheer rock face that climbs out of
the cold waters of the Atlantic Ocean. A narrow ninety-metre
opening allows careful entry to the harbour of St. John's, the
capital of Newfoundland and Labrador. Above the harbour,
from the shops of Water Street to the colorful neighbourhood
clinging to Signal Hill and the suburbs pushing up the Avalon
Peninsula, the crosscurrents of life and work are astir in the city.
It is here that Canada's day begins, hours before most people
have awakened across North America's seven time zones.

It was not always so. Up to the fateful day of March 31, 1949, when Newfoundland became part of Canada, it had for much of its history been a proud but penniless colony, Britain's oldest in North America, unconnected with either the people or the politics of the larger country. The island and its mainland territory of Labrador had been invited to join the other British North American colonies in Confederation in 1867. After sending delegates to both the Charlottetown and Quebec conferences, the old colony backed off from joining the new Dominion. Its folk were fiercely proud, and a Newfoundland ditty of the time went as follows:

> Hurrah for our own native isle, Newfoundland!
> Not a stranger shall own one inch of its strand!
> Her face turns to Britain, her back to the Gulf.
> Come near at your peril, Canadian wolf!

The physical grandeur of Newfoundland and the splendour of its nearly thirty thousand kilometre coastline, the irrepressible character of its people, and its wealth of resources make it a land like no other. The label of *The Rock* fits the place well, and in few other places in the world could a man like Joey Smallwood, driven by impulsiveness, self-assurance, and blind faith, have overcome such obstacles and attained such heights of power as he did here.

Geography, ethnicity, language and religion have produced a Newfoundland that for most of its history has stubbornly resisted the pull of mainstream North American culture. From Inuit migrants of four thousand years ago to the Beothuk hunter-gatherers killed off by white settlers in the nineteenth century, this often inhospitable land has drawn ocean voyagers from time immemorial. The Vikings were here a thousand years ago with their short-lived settlement at L'Anse aux Meadows, today a World Heritage Site. The English, French, and Portuguese fishermen who followed in the wake of John Cabot's 1497 "discovery" treated the waters of Newfoundland as nothing more than a vast cauldron teeming with fish, ready for the taking.

The Newfoundland into which Joseph Roberts Smallwood was born on December 24, 1900, was a country that still lived by the cod, its great ocean resource that the fishing admirals of Great Britain, along with adventurous sailors from many nations, had plundered for more than three hundred years. Generations of Newfoundlanders lived out their lives in tiny outports nestled on the rocky shores of countless fjords and bays that indent the island's coast. Descendants of mostly poor working-class families from the south of Ireland and the west of England, their men fished the icy waters from small dories that either went out on their own, or were launched from banking schooners miles offshore. Equipped only with hand lines and small nets, they returned with plentiful catches that would be smoked and dried, ready for shipment to overseas markets. For thousands of Newfoundland men, the only variation in this dangerous and bitterly hard way of life came in the sealing hunt, which drew fleets of boats to the Icefields every spring, an equally hazardous and uncertain undertaking.

Over all this, during Joey Smallwood's early years, reigned a thin layer of mercantile society, concentrated in the ramshackle seaport of St. John's, whose twenty thousand or so inhabitants boasted of it being the oldest European settlement in North America. Its harbour was filled with vessels from Europe, the United States, and the Caribbean. Its main business street, Water Street, was paved with stone, but most streets were nothing more than dirt passages lined with small wood-frame buildings. The more successful merchants were raising handsome homes on outer streets like King's Bridge Road. They sent their sons to Bishop Field College, an Anglican boarding school on Colonial Street that was the only decent academic institution on the island. In time, it would produce fifteen Rhodes Scholars and an alumnus that would include Joey Smallwood, a student there for five years, his way paid by a generous uncle.

Today, as in Smallwood's time, Newfoundland's population is largely "old stock," ninety-eight per cent English-speaking, but not always in ways readily understood by visitors. Grammar and pronunciation went their own way here, unhindered by the standards of London or New York. The *Dictionary of Newfoundland English* lists hundreds of expressions unique to the island: you can "guttle" your supper (eat greedily), scuff at someone's house (a neighbourhood dance), get bit by a nipper (a large mosquito), or unleash your fance (female dog). Look out if you're told, "The flags are right maggoty here today" — the blackflies are biting. The old dialects, admittedly, are disappearing as Newfoundland's long isolation gives way to the mass culture of an electronic world. It is the conflict between tradition and change that has caused bitter argument in Newfoundland, and it was Joey Smallwood's insistence that Newfoundland give up its old way of life and abandon its prejudices that fuelled the bitterest of struggles.

Newfoundland's descent into bankruptcy is one of the sadder chapters of the depression-ridden 1930s. By then, having attained dominion-status like Canada, Newfoundland was governed by a democratically elected House of Assembly with a Cabinet and a prime minister. In 1934, with Newfoundland unable to meet its obligations, the assembly voted itself out of existence. Britain's colonial office, its name now changed to the Dominions Office, took over and in 1934 appointed a Commission of Government to manage the island's affairs.

Newfoundland's strategic location as a bulwark for North America against possible attack from Nazi Germany brought it into prominence in the Second World War. Britain traded bases in Newfoundland for ships and planes from the United States, and thousands of British, American, and Canadian servicemen brought their paycheques into the island between 1941 and 1945. The end of the war found Newfoundland at a crossroads. Britain could no longer afford to keep up the colony and Newfoundlanders were insistent on regaining control of their own affairs. It was time to decide on the future.

For all the newfound prosperity of wartime, Newfoundland was still desperately poor. Four out of ten of its citizens were functionally illiterate. Not a single university served its population of over three hundred thousand. The island had seventeen dentists and fewer than 150 doctors. Thousands of its outport settlers seldom saw either. Only half of its senior citizens qualified for the six-dollar-a-month old-age pension, and its rate of tuberculosis was the highest in North America. In the words of Joey Smallwood, "We are not a nation, we are a medium-sized municipality left far behind the march of time."

This was the Newfoundland that, together with its mainland territory of Labrador, faced a crucial choice in 1948: to continue with commission government, to reclaim its status as a self-governing dominion and perhaps throw in with the United States — if the Americans would have it — or to join in Confederation with Canada.

Into this maelstrom of uncertainty stepped Joey Smallwood, proffering a dream of unimagined wellbeing and security to a people rich in the traditions of home, family, and church, but bereft of the affluence by then common in the postwar world. Like other young men of colonial upbringing, Smallwood had gone abroad to work and learn and returned home determined to make a difference. For Newfoundland, Smallwood came to believe, economic betterment and democratic rule would be found in union with Canada. In pursuing this goal, he showed himself guilty of the excesses of all men carried off by grand ideas: absolute belief in the rightness of his mission, the conviction that he alone could fulfill it, and the illusion that he would earn the undying gratitude of his countrymen for his efforts.

Twenty years after Newfoundland joined Canada, the prime minister of the day, Pierre Trudeau, said that Joey Smallwood had "changed the destiny of a people, and thereby carved his mark on history." Today, the Newfoundland and Labrador that Trudeau in 1969 described as "a distinct society" (well before the term was applied to Quebec) has transformed itself into an energy power whose economic strength is the envy of the rest of Canada. In examining the life and legacy of Joey Smallwood, one has to ask: How much of Newfoundland's present day confidence can be attributed to what he set in motion? Or did his eagerness to throw in with Canada, combined with his autocratic rule and reckless spending on schemes of doubtful value, lead Newfoundland astray? These are some of the questions to which this book seeks answers. We set out to find them in the thicket of facts, myth, and legend that has grown up around the man remembered as Canada's last Father of Confederation.

All Canadians have an investment in Newfoundland and Labrador, as do the citizens of that province in the rest of their country. It is to a better understanding of each other and to the future of the Canada we share together that this book is dedicated.

1

On the Docks

He stood there alone, clad in a long overcoat, wearing his one and only set of decent clothes — dark-brown Harris tweed trousers soiled from constant use and a Norfolk jacket, topped by a weather-beaten hat. He was at the foot of the gangway to the Bowring Brothers liner SS *Silvia*, a position he found ideal for scrutinizing the faces of passengers leaving the boat. During the three years he'd lived in New York, it had become a weekly ritual for Joey Smallwood to take the ferry across the East River from Manhattan to the Greenpoint docks in Brooklyn, and there to search out newly arriving Newfoundlanders from whom he could obtain the latest homeland gossip.

On this day late in 1923, the air chilled by a North Atlantic breeze, Joey searched for a familiar figure among those departing the *Silvia*, known among Newfoundlanders as a Red Cross liner after the huge red cross of St. George painted on its smokestack.

The symbol, borrowed from the Union Jack, represented the proud English heritage of Bowring Brothers Ltd., the long-established trading company owned by one of the island's wealthiest merchant families.

Possessed still of an innocent face (after all he was only twenty-two), it would be a mistake to think one could read the mind of this young man by just studying his features. On a good day he weighed barely one hundred pounds. His five-foot-four frame hung about him like a wet sack, its starkness relieved only by the piercing blue eyes that stared out from behind thick horn-rimmed glasses. Yet, as those who got to know him soon realized, he carried himself with an air of determination, ready for anything, eager for adventure, with not the slightest doubt that he was up to whatever might face him.

Under his arm, Joey Smallwood carried a large oilcloth map of Newfoundland. He would hail any familiar figure leaving the boat, and if he met someone who was in New York for the first time, if they were not bound for relatives in Brooklyn where some seventy-five thousand Newfoundlanders had settled to work in its shipyards, foundries, and construction jobs, he'd likely take them to his dollar-a-day boarding house at 123 West Fifteenth Street. He favoured it because it was cheap, filled with Newfoundland expatriates, and located a five-minute walk from Union Square, where open-air socialist meetings were an almost daily occurrence.

And the map? It had been drawn by George Turner, the government surveyor, and Joey kept it rolled carefully to protect its ragged edge, the result of being tacked to the walls of more than a few rooms since his departure from St. John's. He seldom allowed it out of his sight, keeping it always with him, even when, as often happened, out of cash or between jobs, he had to sleep on a park bench behind the New York Public Library.

The formative years of Joey Smallwood's early adult life were lived out in New York City between 1920 and 1925. He had gone to New York seeking fame as a journalist and with the idea of possibly settling down there, perhaps even becoming an American citizen. While it is true that Newfoundland kept pulling him back, there is no doubt it was in New York that Joey honed the qualities endowed in him by his family's genes, strengthened by the traits he'd acquired growing up in St. John's, especially during his five years at the leading Church of England school on the island, Bishop Feild College.

Rubbing shoulders at the boarding school with the sons of wealthy merchants, he developed a healthy contempt for economic injustice and embraced socialism as a solution to the world's ills. He became an avid reader, developing a lifelong insistence on having something in his hand to read, providing it taught him something interesting, and he was interested in most things. His self-confidence skyrocketed, and he felt inferior to no one, an attitude that would enable him to approach anyone anywhere, no matter their prominence or wealth. Joey, in brief, was growing into the strong-willed man who would come to see his destiny as indissoluble from that of his beloved Newfoundland.

Joey's years at Feild College, he would come to realize, set his course in life. He would never have gone there but for the generosity of his uncle, Fred Smallwood, who decided Joey should have the best education Newfoundland could provide. At first, he had trouble fitting in, the poorest boy from the poorest family. His weekly ten cent allowance, provided by Uncle Fred on top of Joey's $37.50 per year tuition and board bill, usually dribbled to just a few cents by the time the Headmaster had deducted fines for various misdemeanors. He was a troublemaker from the start. He promoted his first strike when he campaigned for more molasses on the bread pudding students were fed, then led a boycott of the dining room over punishments handed out for skipping church. He became a Boy Scout, neglected athletics, but surpassed his classmates in Latin, French, and English. He came second in a British Empire essay contest on "Duty to the Empire." With the First World War (or the Great War, as it was then known) raging in Europe, Joey and his friends snuck out of the school to watch soldiers of the Newfoundland Regiment drill at Quidi Vidi Lake. This was when Joey first dreamt his dream to be Prime Minister of Newfoundland.

Joey left Bishop Field under a cloud, giving up friendships with boys who would reach the top in Newfoundland politics and society, little knowing that he would be right up there with them. The cause of his departure in the spring of 1916 was a quarrel with a housemaster over a disturbance in class. The tiff was insignificant in itself, but symbolic of Joey's fierce resistance to anything he regarded as unjust. His academic marks had been strong, those for character unacceptably low. He was fifteen, his formal education at an end, equivalent to grade ten by today's standards. After a night spent sleeping on a bag of wood chips in one of the school's outbuildings, he confessed to his Uncle Fred what had happened. He was unsuitable for school, and unsuitable for employment in the family's boot and shoe factory. He'd have to make his way on his own.

Joey Smallwood always retained his affinity for the outports of Newfoundland, even though it would be one of his great goals as premier to relocate the inhabitants of the poorest and least-favoured settlements to larger centres. He boasted of having been born in one: the small town of Gambo on Bonavista Bay, the great indentation in the northeast or "English Coast" of Newfoundland.

Joey Smallwood, second from the left in the front row, with his fellow young men of Bishop Feild College, circa 1913.

Gambo was more a forestry than a fishing settlement, and the fact his family moved from there to St. John's when Joey was six months old did not lessen his lifelong connection with that community.* His claim to be a "bayman" when he was more a "townie" is just one of the many contradictions of Joey Smallwood's life.

Joey was the first child of thirteen born to his mother, the former Minnie May DeVannah, and Charles Smallwood, having come into the world on December 24, 1900. His grandfather David Smallwood named him Joseph Roberts, after two men he greatly admired — Joseph Chamberlain, the British secretary of state for the colonies, and Field Marshall Lord Roberts, commander of British troops in the South African War.

---

* His life is memorialized in the J.R. Smallwood Interpretation Centre in Gambo, containing artifacts and exhibits. It opened in 1999, the 50th anniversary of Newfoundland's entry into Confederation.

David and Julia Smallwood and family, circa 1885.

The Smallwoods were relative latecomers to Newfoundland, Joey's grandfather having arrived there in 1861 from Prince Edward Island. David was descended from Joseph Smallwood, a master mariner born in Virginia but caught up in the American Revolutionary War. Loyal to the Crown, he fled to England and in 1783 received a grant of land in Prince Edward Island. In Newfoundland, he opened a sawmill and later launched a shoemaking business that would become the main supplier of leather footwear for the island's fishermen. David was clever marketer, and the fame of the business spread when he had a sign in the shape of a giant black boot hung from a twelve-foot iron bar drilled into the rock at the entrance to St. John's harbour. On it was painted the command BUY SMALLWOOD'S BOOTS.

Joey's father, Charles, rebelled against work in the family business and instead set out to become a lumber surveyor.

He had tried his luck in Boston, returned home disillusioned, and took up drink. Joey's childhood was filled with scenes of his drunken father crashing about the house or lying abed, sodden from rum and whisky, his mother Minnie May trying desperately to sober him up. Her struggle to keep her husband out of the grasp of the bottle was probably a factor in her giving up her Roman Catholic faith and turning to the more stridently anti-liquor Pentecostal Church. Remembrance of the dreadful scenes of his father's drunkenness kept Joey away from hard liquor all his life, although he did try — without success — to fatten himself up with a bottle of beer a day, and he would eventually learn to enjoy wine and port.

Cut off from the family business, Charles and Minnie May raised Joey and his sisters and brothers in a state of near poverty. Between binges, Charles ran a carting business, lugging goods about St. John's in horse-drawn wagons. When Joey was seven, the family left a succession of ever-draftier rented houses to take up residence on Southside Road on the edge of St. John's. Living there, they were looked on as "country people" and even spoke differently than townsfolk. Charles had managed to scrabble together the few hundred dollars needed to purchase a piece of land 150 feet wide that extended 2,000 feet up the hillside. Joey and his brother Reginald led their horse up the steep hill to cut wood for their stoves. Minnie May planted a large garden and kept hens as well as a pig or two. Joey was careful to absent himself when it came time to slaughter a hog, and once away from home, he never ate fresh pork.

Joey's decision to leave Feild College and his unwillingness to return to a crowded, squalling household left him but one option:

find a job and a place away from home. He settled into a room in his grandfather's house on Springdale Street and went job hunting. With the war on, workers were in demand and Joey had no trouble catching on as an apprentice at the *Plaindealer*, one of the many small sheets published in St. John's. Unfortunately, the arrival of a typesetting machine put him out of work. He went to the *Spectator*, another tiny sheet, as a printer's devil at two dollars a week, but the paper soon folded. This was followed by a year in the printing department of the town's leading newspaper, the *Daily News*, before he became a bill collector in the circulation department. In October 1918, he spotted an ad for a reporter at the *St. John's Evening Telegram*. Joey felt fully qualified; he'd had an article about his idol, Fishermen's Union founder William Coaker, published in the *Fishermen's Advocate*. He got the job at the *Telegram*. What an opportunity! It was a Liberal paper, and a chance to become a real journalist.

Joey's first big scoop as a reporter came on the morning of June 30, 1919, when he noticed two ships of the Royal Navy anchored in the harbour. Disguised as a secretary to an official of the Newfoundland Constabulary, he got himself aboard HMS *Cornwall*. The *Cornwall* sailed into Bonavista Bay, where the captain announced a raid on an illegal distillery on Flat Island. A machine gun was mounted in a cutter and a hundred sailors and policeman, accompanied by Smallwood, set out through the mists. Joey wrote in his dispatch that "dozens of desperate men armed with sealing guns and fowling pieces" lay in wait behind the rocks. In fact, most of the moonshiners had gone fishing, but his story helped sell hundreds of extra papers that night.

A more substantial assignment involved the first transatlantic flights that were about to take place between Newfoundland and Ireland. Great crowds turned out to watch the comings

The intrepid Smallwood as a reporter, circa 1919.

and goings. With many competing flights to cover, Smallwood chose to go to Harbour Grace, where Royal Navy vice admiral Mark Kerr was readying a giant Handley Page for its flight. The young reporter should have stayed in St. John's: while watching mechanics work on Kerr's plane, he heard the news that two other Britons, Captain Jack Alcock and Lieutenant "Teddy" Brown, had taken off. Sixteen hours later, on June 15, 1919, they landed their Vimy bomber in an Irish bog, completing the first non-stop transatlantic flight.

Joey Smallwood was reading omnivorously, pursuing his cousin Dot Vincent — who worked in a record store across the street from the *Telegram* — and getting himself involved in unions and politics. He joined Newfoundland's largest union, the Newfoundland Industrial Workers' Association, and became the volunteer editor of its paper, the *Industrial Worker*. He had less success with Dot, who moved to Montreal.

In the 1919 Newfoundland election, still too young to vote, Joey worked for a fledgling Workingmen's Party that failed to elect its three St. John's candidates. His *Telegram* salary had reached the unimaginable level of twenty-five dollars a week, but by now he was thinking beyond the narrow strictures of his daily beat. He coaxed *Telegram* publisher William Herder into giving him a letter of introduction to the publisher of the *Halifax Herald*. With that, and a free pass on the Newfoundland Railway that took him across the island — the first time he'd travelled by train — Joey bid adieu to his first real newspaper job.

At the station, where his family had gathered to see him off, he was approached by a group of Jews. They presented him with a bouquet of flowers. Joey had operated as a freelance publicity agent while working at the *Telegram*, and their tribute was perhaps due to some favourable publicity he would have arranged. At a time of virulent anti-Semitism, Smallwood had demonstrated his respect for everyone he met; it was an attitude that would allow him to develop lasting relationships with Jewish friends he'd make in the Socialist community in New York City.

Joey Smallwood saw Halifax as a stepping stone to New York, his real goal. He was taken on immediately at the *Herald*, but Halifax had lapsed into a sleepy seaport at the end of the war, and he had few exciting stories to cover. After several months he quit, took the train to Yarmouth, and boarded the overnight ferry for Boston.

He easily passed cursory scrutiny by the U.S. Immigration Service. He answered honestly that he had no job to go to and learned this was the secret to getting into the country. Immigration officials were under orders to turn back anyone who claimed to have employment awaiting them. Immigration gangs were known to be operating, selling innocent newcomers on the fiction that for a price, they could set them up with a job in advance.

Boston was the biggest city young Smallwood had yet encountered, and he ran into difficulty on his first day. He'd been given the address of a boarding house at 8 Allston Street, which he'd been told was just behind nearby Scollay Square. After half an hour in a taxi, he noticed the metre was showing six dollars and they still hadn't gotten there. Joey spotted a policeman, ordered the driver to stop, and told the officer of his plight. The driver claimed he'd been told to go to the suburban town of Allston, not 8 Allston Street. The policeman sided with Joey and sent the driver back into Boston. When they reached their destination, Joey tried to pay in Canadian money. "That money is no good," the driver asserted. He offered to take it at fifty cents on the dollar. Not one to be trifled with, Joey marched into the closest bank, changed his money, and paid off the driver.

The next day, Smallwood visited the *Boston Herald-Traveler*, where he asked the city editor, a man named O'Brien, for a job. The editor guessed he was a Canadian, and Joey quickly corrected him (Newfoundland was still decades away from Confederation). Joey was hired, and his first assignment was to wander the Boston Common, the great park in the heart of the city, and write his impressions of the many stump orators who were holding forth, often from soap boxes, with their views of American politics. He was particularly impressed by a speaker who was promoting the Socialist Labor Party. After the speaker was finished, Joey interviewed him and found out he was from St. John's and was the son of a devout Irish Ronan Catholic. Joey mentioned that the man's father would be horrified if he knew his son was preaching socialism. "He knows, and you're absolutely right," the speaker told Joey.

Joey liked Boston, but two months of routine assignments bored him. The ticket he'd bought in Halifax had New York as its destination. It was time to use it.

2

At the Beck of the Call

The idea of becoming a reporter for the *New York Evening Call*, the famous Socialist organ, had blazed in Joey Smallwood's brain almost from the moment of landing his first newspaper job in St. John's. Yes, he wanted American experience — that would help him when he got back home — but most of all, it was his dream to be part of the great Socialist movement that he believed, as an idealistic youth, held the answers to all the problems of mankind.

The train from Boston disgorged its passengers at Grand Central Station, a confusing enough place for even the most blasé travellers to New York. For a nineteen-year-old from Newfoundland, the noise and congestion of the crowded station might have been enough to cause panic, but Joey revelled in the movement of commuters and the shouts of ticket agents and assorted peddlers. He made his way triumphantly through the concourse and, on reaching 42nd Street, decided he would to try to walk all over Manhattan.

Joey found his way to the offices of the *Call*, in a dingy loft of an old downtown factory building. He was desperate for a job, not only to fulfill his dream but because he was paying the way for a Newfoundland friend he'd roomed with in Boston, Andrew Lehr. He'd insisted on coming with him to New York and Joey was already running low on money. The city editor of the *Call* was a crusty one-time book editor named Louis Baury. Whether he took pity on Smallwood, or saw in him an ardent young Socialist who would produce the kind of copy favoured by the paper's owners, the Workingman's Cooperative Publishing Association, he hired him on the spot.

As Joey wandered through the newsroom, one of the first men he met was a fellow Newfoundlander, also from St. John's. Gerald Fitzgibbon turned out to be a man of many talents — he was a hypnotist-magician, a cross-country runner, and a great Socialist stump speaker at rallies held in New York parks. One day, Fitzgibbon invited Joey and other newsmen to come to the East River to witness a daring feat. He had himself bound in chains, sealed in a canvas bag, and thrown into the water. "My God, Gerry," Joey exclaimed, "suppose you don't come up?" But within a couple of minutes, Fitzgibbon did come up, and he garnered much publicity for his accomplishment.

New York in 1920 was on the verge of the greatest economic boom in American history. The decade that would become known as the Roaring Twenties would end in the stock market crash of 1929 and open the way to the Great Depression of the 1930s. All that was in the future, however, and the editors of the *Call* were struggling to keep their paper going. Its circulation was dropping like a stone and was down to twenty thousand a day when Joey was hired. The *Call's* anti-war stance had cost it its second-class mailing privileges in 1917, making subscriptions prohibitively expensive. As well, the country was caught up in anti-Communist hysteria following the Russian Revolution, and anything that smacked of communism or socialism was suspect.

On May Day, 1919, a mob of veterans inflamed by the Red Scare had barged into the *Call's* offices, burnt books and pamphlets, and beaten up seven members of the staff. The great Eugene Debs, Socialist Party candidate for president in 1920, was in jail for opposing the wartime draft and had to campaign from behind bars. He collected nearly a million votes, but a Republican, Warren G. Harding, was elected on the promise of a "return to normalcy" after the sacrifices of war. Americans were rapidly losing interest in socialism, convinced that the rising stock market promised prosperity for all — "a chicken in every pot and a car in every garage."*

Joey Smallwood was sent to interview a medley of interesting newsmakers: capitalists and labor union organizers, artists and writers, advocates for black equality, and crusaders for freedom of speech. He was in the crowd, notebook in hand, at Madison Square Garden the night Eugene Debs addressed twenty thousand roaring supporters following his release from prison. Joey became familiar with Harlem, the New York district where blacks had been settling for the past twenty years. He felt comfortable in their midst, and it was there he met Marcus Garvey, who would become famous for his futile efforts to encourage blacks to return to Africa. Many black leaders shared Garvey's view that Africa offered a better future for their race than any that might be found in America. Joey wrote of Garvey's

---

* Herbert Hoover would campaign for the Republicans on this slogan in 1928, handily winning the presidency.

plan to set up a Black Cross Steamship Line that would facilitate such a migration. Garvey had managed to purchase a boat that he moored in the East River, where he charged a dollar to go aboard and look around. Thousands did, but no ship of the Black Line ever sailed to Africa. Joey thought Garvey to be one of the most dynamic people he'd ever met, but ahead of his time.

Joey's colleagues at the *Call* were an eclectic lot. He arrived too late to meet John Reed, author of *Ten Days That Shook the World*, a book on the 1917 Russian Revolution. Among the staff who addressed one another as "Comrade," Joey especially enjoyed the fellowship of Richard Rohman — a promising young playwright — and Philip Hochstein, who would become a powerhouse in one of America's biggest newspaper chains. There was no class distinction at the *Call*, and Joey spent his leisure hours with his "comrades" eating at economical restaurants like The Three Steps Down and, on occasion, the more costly Café Royale.

After little more than a year in New York, Smallwood felt the urge to go home. He took a leave of absence from the *Call* late in 1921 and headed back to St. John's with his friend Andrew Lehr. The House of Assembly was in session, and Joey covered the debates for the St. John's newspapers. Early in the New Year, he talked his way into a free trip to New York on the tramp steamer *Yankton*. Joey recalls in his memoirs that, with nothing to do but read, he devoured Theodore Dreiser's *Sister Carrie*, Gustave Flaubert's *Madame Bovary*, and Herman Sudermann's *Song of Songs* — all having the same theme of women seeking escape from narrow, provincial lives.

Back in New York, Joey decided his talents deserved a better outlet than the *Call*. Charles R. Miller, the editor-in-chief of the *New York Times*, had vacationed in Newfoundland a couple of years before, at which time Joey had interviewed him. Miller had liked the story so much he ordered a dozen copies and gave Joey a fulsome letter of introduction. Joey took the letter to Carr van Anda, managing editor of the *Times*, who told him, "Young man, do you realize how fortunate you are to have a letter like this from Mr. Miller?" Van Anda said the paper had a waiting list of a thousand applicants, but promised Joey he could start work in a few weeks.

The "few weeks" of idle waiting brought Joey to his lowest point in New York. He could no longer afford his six-dollar-a-week rooming house. Leaving his belongings for safekeeping, he struck out with a razor and the clothes on his back, spending several nights at a fifty-cent flop house. Deciding he couldn't afford even that, he found something cheaper — a place near the Bowery where one floor had been divided into cubicles by chicken wire. There was no privacy, and tenants were kicked out at seven o'clock in the morning. Joey would go to a public washroom, find a cheap café for a ten-cent breakfast, and wait for the opening of the public library.

To fill his time one day, Joey decided to look up a Canadian filmmaker, Ernest Shipman, who he had heard was in New York. Shipman had made several successful movies based on Ralph Connor's romanticized novels of Canadian life, including *Cameron of the Royal Mounted*. Joey got Shipman's address from the telephone directory and went to his office. They got on well, and Shipman explained his new moviemaking strategy. He was producing a series of films on Canadian cities, financed by local businessmen. When Joey suggested he make a movie on Newfoundland, Shipman offered him a job as an advance agent, tasked with putting together a group that would be interested in hearing Shipman's proposition. The lure of being involved in moviemaking, combined with the offer of an immediate salary, was more appealing than waiting for the *Times*.

Joey took the next boat back to Newfoundland. There, he arranged for Shipman to meet with local businessmen. The meeting seemed a success; Shipman enjoyed a night of trout fishing in the pouring rain and urged Joey to go on to other Maritime provinces to organize similar meetings. Joey lined up potential backers in Halifax, Fredericton, and Charlottetown, with the upshot that he found himself squiring Shipman's favourite scenario writer, Faith Green — a woman in her late fifties — about Prince Edward Island. "We must have been the strangest team of movie-writers," Joey would later recall in his memoirs. Sadly, none of the movies were made, and Joey decided to return to New York.

Joey was too embarrassed to go back to the *Times*. By now, the *Call* had finally closed, re-emerging as the weekly *New Leader*. It couldn't pay Joey enough to live on, and he supplemented his income with a ten-dollar-a-week job with the Socialist Party, going around to the parks and speaking to whatever crowds he could gather. Most of his salary came from the collection plate he passed after each speech. He also worked for several trade magazines before landing a job with the Gilliams Editorial Syndicate, where he dreamt up ideas for illustrated stories he wrote for Sunday newspapers around the United States.

When the 1924 presidential election came along, Joey was sent to eighteen cities throughout New York to speak on behalf of the Socialist Party. At one point, he even tried to start his own newspaper, getting out one issue before realizing he wouldn't be able to make a go of it. He tried other lines of work, too. He spent an excruciating few days polishing lengths of rusted railway track on a giant emery wheel. Another job took him below decks of ships docked at Staten Island to clean the ships' engines of grease. But the pattern of his life for the next twenty years — a combination of newspapering, unionizing, and politicking — had been put firmly in place.

Ever since arriving in New York, Joey had been a steady customer of the New York Public Library, while still accumulating as many books as he could afford to buy. He read biographies about great leaders, books on anarchism and socialism, and classical and popular works. He selected a different church to visit every week and over a year listened to the wisdom of Christian ministers, Jewish rabbis, and Muslim imams. He joined the Socialist Party and took out a membership at a debating society called the Civic Club.

It was this drive for knowledge — or perhaps the normal desire of a young man to meet girls — that led Smallwood to enroll in the Rand School of Social Science. It was an offshoot of the Socialist Party, set up to educate workers, serve as a research bureau, and run summer camps for socialists and trade union activists. At the Rand School, Joey found himself entranced by young ladies in short skirts, with rouged knees and bobbed hair. He hadn't seen much of that back in St. John's. Of all the sights in New York, he wrote in one piece, the girls "are perhaps the most interesting of all." One time, he was taken to a theatre to watch tryouts by forty or fifty girls vying for chorus line jobs, and he couldn't understand why the director had hired not a single one of them. He later watched a performance of the *Ziegfeld Follies* and realized that to make it into a New York chorus line a young woman had to have almost perfect looks, body coordination, and grace.

A reading of the surviving half-dozen letters written to or by Joey suggests he had several affairs, all of them ending, if not in unhappiness, at least in disappointment. Probably, all these liaisons involved girls he met at the Rand School, where Jewish girls were predominant among the 1,500 or so students. Joey had become such a familiar face to people in the Jewish ghetto of the Lower East Side that many assumed he was also Jewish. Perhaps his looks — his dark hair, hooked nose, and horn rimmed spectacles — helped convey that impression.

In May 1923, on an outing to the New Jersey farm of a Rand School professor, Joey made the acquaintance of a beautiful dark-haired girl. Lillian Zahn was an eighteen-year-old student at New York University. Her parents were Jewish refugees from Galicia who followed Orthodox practices, and Lillian, like many first-generation Jewish Americans, was in rebellion against the old ways. Joey took a picture of Lillian and sent it to her, along with a short note. When he received no answer, he wrote again. She replied, "Since you are not a New Yorker, you must be an interesting personality to meet. You see, I am so tired of New Yorkers that it is a relief to meet someone from elsewhere. If you will wait for me in front of the Rand School Saturday, June 2 at 7 p.m., we may have an opportunity to hear each other's ideas." A daring suggestion coming from a woman, although Lillian's reference to sharing ideas gives the note a respectable cover.

Around the time Joey met Lillian, he had been in touch with another young woman, known to us only by her first name, Cynthia. On June 12, 1923, she wrote to Joey to thank him for his "sweet letter" and to tell him that while he was out of the city on an assignment she "didn't have a friend in the world." She went on: "I was so glad to hear you say that you wanted to get back ... I dared to believe that I had something to look forward to." Another girl, Helen, wrote him on the letterhead of the *Literary Digest*, a leading magazine of the time, to reproach him for suggesting his handwriting would have been hard to read. "How can you say that your writing is so terrible? Why, I would read it if it took me all day."

Joey's interest, however, was by now totally focused on Lillian Zahn. He had fallen head over heels in love. The two were suddenly inseparable. Lillian enjoyed cultural events and that summer they took in plays, concerts, and art showings. They also had fun at Coney Island rides and held hands in Central Park. On July 30, Lillian sent a note addressed to "my dear Joseph." The next Wednesday, she suggested, they could "go to the opera at Polo Grounds, or to the Stadium concert." She added, "Please find out about either," and passed on the good news that she'd secured "a fine position in a weekly publication as stenographer and secretary on 42 St." They were to meet at 7:15, and she hoped he would "not forget to bring the two books" they loved.

This was no mere summer romance, however. When Joey returned to Newfoundland late that year on work for the Fishermen's Union, he kept up a regular flow of letters describing his work and expressing his love. On December 4, in a two-page typewritten letter addressed to "My own dear Lillie," he spoke of planning to write a history of the Fishermen's Union. It would run to four hundred thousand words, and he hoped to have it published in New York, where he was soon to return. He closed: "With all the love in the world, as always." Having made a carbon copy of the letter for his files, he signed it Joe and surrounded his name with a dozen *x*'s. Their affair, however, seems to have ended shortly after his return early in 1924. Lillian had tried to teach Joey Yiddish, apparently believing she might pass him off to her family as an English Jew. According to Smallwood biographer Richard Gwyn, Joey became stage struck when Lillian introduced him to her mother. He could only bow and smile. "I know he's a goy," her mother declared. "You can't fool me. He's a goy." They never saw each other again.*

For a young Newfoundlander without experience in such matters, the objections of Lillian's family must have been hard to understand. Yet the unhappy disruption of this relationship did not discourage Joey from conducting a tempestuous affair with Sophie Abrams, whom he'd likely also met through the Rand School. Letters went back and forth between them, but those that have been preserved are filled with misunderstanding and frustration. On November 20, 1924, she left a note under Joey's door asking for a meeting at five o'clock. It may have been their first written contact, as she confessed she was "taking a good deal for granted, making a supposition that you want to talk to me." She was being forward, to say the least. Their meeting must have led to a misunderstanding, because four days later, Sophie was demanding Joey return pictures she had given him, as "photographs should be given to friends only." There would be no need for him to write back — he need only put the pictures in "the stamped envelope enclosed herewith." Obviously, there'd been a lovers' quarrel. But worse was to come. Trying to make things right, Joey had gone to her house and rang the doorbell but failed to get an answer. He then wrote to her. She replied on November 28, saying the doorbell had been out of order and that if he had knocked, she would have answered. She added that their letters must have crossed in the mail, and confessed contritely that hers had been "written at white heat."

---

* Lillian Zahn became a Yiddish folk singer, and in 1948, when Joey Smallwood was campaigning in the Newfoundland referendums, she made her first visit to Canada, performing all summer at the Hakoah Country Club on Trout Lake near Ste. Agathe, Quebec.

Things seemed to settle down, but it was not long before Sophie wrote to end their relationship:

> After much contemplation I have come to the conclusion that a frank letter would be of mutual benefit. I can not see you any more for several reasons. One is that my mother wants me all to herself, another reason is that I care for you too much to see you repeatedly and be absolutely void of all feeling for you.

The anguish that these contradictory sentiments suggest is reinforced by Sophie's closing words: "Let me impress upon you, my dear Joe, that it is not without regret (aye, more than that) that I close." Sophie's allusion to her mother raises the likelihood that her family, like Lillian's, objected to her seeing a gentile boy.

Joey had learned that girls liked him, but the fact that affairs with young Jewish women could go nowhere must have filled him with sadness. He perhaps sought advice from his landlady on West Fifteenth Street, Mrs. Taylor, whom he had come to regard almost as a mother. He'd also become friendly with her son Arthur, with whom he doubtless shared his distress. Joey's disappointments in his romantic life in New York probably became a factor in his decision to return to Newfoundland for good.

If not a success in love, Joey Smallwood was a success in his newspaper work in New York. He'd survived the folding of the *Call*, had managed to make several trips back home, but had also gotten to know and interview many luminaries of American politics and society. These included Clarence Darrow, a brilliant criminal lawyer; the charismatic Fiorello LaGuardia, future mayor of New York; Mrs. Eleanor Roosevelt, a future president's wife; the famous muckraker Lincoln Steffans; the eminent (and eccentric) economist Thorstein Veblen; and Frank A. Vanderlip, probably the leading American banker of the 1920s. His years in New York, Smallwood would remember, were "glorious and exciting and wonderful."

3

A Yearning for Home

Sometime early in 1925, Joey Smallwood came to the realization that it was in Newfoundland that his future lay. There was nothing to hold him in New York. Having grown up poor, a witness to the hardships besetting the island, he could no longer resist his yearning to do something to improve the lives of his countrymen. When John P. Burke, head of the International Brotherhood of Pulp, Sulphite, and Paper Mill Workers, invited Joey to go to Newfoundland to reorganize a faltering branch of the union, he found himself at a turning point in his life.

Joey thought of John Burke as one of the greatest of American trade union leaders. That put him almost on a par with his idol William F. Coaker, the founding leader of the Newfoundland Fishermen's Union. Joey had met Burke as a reporter for the *Call*, and the two often went for long walks. That winter, the fate of Pulp, Sulphite local 63 in Grand Falls, Newfoundland, was much on Burke's mind. Following a bitter strike, the union had lost many of its members to a rival, the Canadian-based Paper Makers' union, and it needed shaking up. As well, there was a chance to organize a new local in Corner Brook, where a new pulp and newsprint mill was about to start up. Burke offered Joey forty-five dollars a week — more money than he'd ever made in New York — to return to Newfoundland and take on the both tasks. Joey agreed, but told Burke he intended to work on another project at the same time. He had a scheme to unite all the various unions of Newfoundland — miners, pulp workers, fishermen, and railway workers — into a Newfoundland Federation of Labour. Properly organized, Joey thought, they'd be able to improve the wages of all union workers, which were currently not much above subsistence levels. Burke reluctantly went along with Joey's grand plan.

Smallwood's powers of persuasion soon had the Grand Falls workers back into the fold of the Paper, Sulphite union. He started his federation by enrolling six unions as members and got himself elected president. Then he set off for Corner Brook to organize workers at the new pulp mill. The social highlight of the week in that raw forestry town was the Sunday afternoon arrival of the train from St. John's. Joey decided to go where the people were. Standing on an oil drum on the station platform, he'd hold forth on the benefits of the union. Within a few months, Joey would remember, "Local 64 was well and truly laid and fairly set on its course." His labour federation, however, fared less well. Without his presence in Grand Falls to keep things together, it soon floundered and Joey had to give up his scheme to organize "one big union" in Newfoundland.

A distraction entered Joey's life at this time. He'd taken a room at a boarding house in Curling, three miles along the railway from Corner Brook. The landlady was Mrs. Serena Baggs, the widow of a sea captain. She had two daughters. But it was Mrs. Baggs's young cousin Clara Isobel Oates, visiting from Carbonear on the other side of the island, who caught Joey's eye.

Despite their differing backgrounds — Joey now a worldly journalist and union organizer and Clara the shy daughter of a fisherman — the two soon found they shared common interests. She was twenty-three and Joey was twenty-five. Clara's fondness for reading and her passion for the intimate details of the lives of British royalty were matched by Joey's appetite for books and his unbounded interest in all manner of subjects. The fact she was good looking, with bright blue eyes and long hair that she sometimes let fall over her shoulders, didn't hurt, either. On top of that, Clara was gifted musically and had studied piano in Nova Scotia. On Sunday evenings, she would play the piano and sing for the residents of the boardinghouse.

Joey Smallwood was used to doing things in a hurry, and barely six weeks after their meeting, he asked Clara to be his wife. She agreed, and their wedding was set for November 23, 1925, at Carbonear. That left him a few months to tackle other projects.

One day, while walking the railway line from his boarding house to town, he encountered a gang of men repairing the track. They were section workers: men responsible for maintaining a section of the track, usually seven to ten miles long. Working in all weather, it was their job to repair bridges and culverts, replace worn ties, hammer in loose spikes, and pack down the gravel under the rails — tasks vital to the safe running of the trains. The men lived with their families in little cottages, usually not much more than shacks, alongside the tracks. When they found out Joey had made a union in Corner Brook for the paper workers, they tackled him about forming one for themselves. They told him their pay was about to be cut from twenty-five cents an hour to twenty-two and one-half cents. "Us fellers, section-men, we got no union."

Joey and his wife, Clara, with their child Ramsay in 1926.

Joey's decision to take up the cause of the section-men plunged him into one of the most exciting episodes of his life, and one he would talk about for years to come. He took a train to the end of the line at Channel-Port aux Basques, and signed up the workers there, collecting a fifty cent fee from each of them. He dashed off a quick letter to Clara to tell her he had been "infernally busy." Then, he set out to walk the full distance of the main line, as well as several branch lines between there and St. John's — a distance of seven hundred and forty-seven miles in all. It took him three pairs of boots, but by the middle of October he had reached Carbonear, where he was reunited with Clara and arrangements were made for their wedding. He was on the last leg of his trek to St. John's when he encountered an incoming freight train at the Avondale station, thirty-six miles out of the capital. It had a passenger car attached to it, and Joey, standing at the door to the station, saw three men descend and come toward him. One turned out to be Herbert J. Russell, general manager of the Newfoundland Railway. They'd read of Joey's walk and Russell quickly recognized who they'd encountered. A discussion ensued. Joey told them every single section-man but one had joined his union, and he could close down the railway at any time. It was a brave line but Russell, knowing that a strike by maintenance workers would stop the trains, agreed on the spot to rescind the wage cut.

Realizing he would soon be a married man, Joey had to think about his future. He had, in effect, worked himself out of a job. He'd achieved his goal for the section-men, and the Sulphite, Paper union was doing all right without him. How was he going to support a wife? He would start a newspaper — what else?

Joey got off a letter to Clara, but there was little in it of a romantic nature. He told her he was sure they would be happy together, and further wrote:

> You are a little brick. Now, about getting married. The convention [of the union] is the 18th. I want to be there for the opening … I want to get the first issue of paper out, and have second on the way … I might go over to Carbonear on Sunday or Monday morning … Anyway, suppose we plan to get married on Monday the 22nd? I'll manage my end of it OK. Please, sweetheart, write immediately.

Years later, Joey would write in his memoirs:

> My marriage ... was one of the most fortunate
> events of my life, though perhaps not always
> of hers ... She has been the soul of loyalty
> from that moment, a helpmeet in the sincerest
> meaning of the word, a loyal and loving wife,
> and a wonderful mother.

Settling his bride into a tiny flat in St. John's, Joey arranged for his new paper, the *Labour Outlook*, to be printed by a local Liberal Party daily, the *Globe*. His first subscribers would be the six hundred section-men who had each paid him fifty cents. They'd get the paper as a free bonus. It soon became apparent to the owner of the *Globe*, who was about to lose his regular editor, that Joey would make an excellent replacement. A deal was made for Joey to close his paper and take the editorship. His best efforts, however, were not enough to keep the *Globe* afloat. It folded six months later. During that time, Joey had set to work on another project, to publish a Newfoundland *Who's Who*. He formed a fifty-fifty partnership with a printer, Dick Hibbs, but with the loss of his *Globe* salary, Joey was without funds. He sold his half to Hibbs, who went on to bring out several handsome editions.

An ordinary man would have cast about for another job in St. John's, but Joey Smallwood was no ordinary man. It was time to broaden his experience, and he'd do it through a visit to England. Joey gave a little money to Clara, who went home to Carbonear, and he sailed to Liverpool, where he took a train to London. It was an exciting time for a Socialist to visit Britain. The Labour Party had won a minority in the House of Commons and its leader, Ramsay MacDonald, was the new prime minister.

Joey haunted the House of Commons listening to the debates when he was not seated in the British Library, his nose in a book. He picked up a few extra pounds writing articles for political magazines and sold some pictures of Newfoundland to a London newspaper. In three days and nights of non-stop effort, he wrote his first book, *Coaker of Newfoundland*, a biography of his hero William Coaker. The Labour Publishing Company managed to sell several thousand copies.

With Joey in England, Clara had a lonely Christmas in 1926. He took Christmas dinner by himself at a Lyons Corner House in London, also feeling lonely. Clara's letters to Joey betray her bitterness and disappointment. There was the new baby, Ramsay, to look after, and he had gone away without her. It was especially galling that he had gone alone to the country whose kings and queens she had spent a lifetime reading about and had longed to visit. "I can't remember when I spent such a lonely Xmas," Clara wrote. "I had not a cent as you know for Xmas, not a cent to give for collection when I went to church." She added:

> I don't know how some would act or what they would say or do if they were left as I am and had to put up with what I have. I have got through, God knows.... When I needed your help most you failed me then and if you fail in everything else it does not matter. I will not reprove you for it if you were to meet ill luck and come back again without a cent.

This was Clara's third letter to Joey in England, and it upset and angered him. Replying from his Bloomsbury rooming house, he told her, "This was the last thing I expected from you.

The whole tone of it was bitter and nasty, and it made me feel pretty bad. God knows I want to hear from you, and often, but not that kind of letter."

Referring to difficulties they must have had early in their marriage, Joey expressed his frustrations with Clara:

> [You] sounded just the same as the talk you used to use before baby was born. Just when I was feeling more love and tenderness for you than any time before you have to write this kind of letter to me. It was like a cold dash of water in the face ... You mustn't run away with the idea that everything is a bed of roses here for me. It is not. I have got so thin you would hardly know me. People remark it to me, and I have to tell them that I have been sick. At the present moment I have about eight shillings to my name and my room is paid until Tuesday.

Joey ended his litany of problems by assuring Clara, "There is lots of love and life and happiness ahead for us yet."

The spring of 1927 brought good news for Newfoundland when Britain's Privy Council — the arbiter of colonial disputes — rejected Quebec's claim to Labrador. The year was notable for other reasons. Charles Lindbergh made his solo flight of the Atlantic in the *Spirit of St. Louis*, the first phone call was placed between New York and London, and Hollywood gave birth to the Academy Awards. The year also brought Joey Smallwood home again to Newfoundland.

Joey's interests were by now evolving, and he was beginning to weigh up the failures of his past against his hopes for the future. Still a Socialist at heart, he had come to realize he would need another political horse to ride if he ever hoped to fulfill his boyhood dream of becoming prime minister; the Liberal Party stood the closest to his political ideals. Its leader, Sir Richard Squires, once disgraced by scandal but now back as head of the Opposition, was likely to win the next election, set for the fall of 1928. If Joey was to be part of that campaign, he had to play his cards carefully.

Joey headed straight for his old stamping ground of Corner Brook, with the idea of starting a newspaper to compete with the *Western Star*, owned by the paper company. He raised money from mill workers and launched the *Humber Herald*. Before long, it had over two thousand paying subscribers. Joey ordered a printing press and a linotype machine from Toronto. All this, of course, was intended to pave the way for his getting the Liberal nomination in the Humber riding. Joey kept Sir Richard informed of his progress, boasting he was building the best Liberal machine on the island. His reward was a letter from Squires that Joey would never forget. It told him Squires had decided he must himself run in Humber, and he wanted Joey as his campaign manager. The letter filled Joey with anger and disappointment. He stormed from the *Herald* office and set off on a ten-mile walk to the next railway station and back. By then, he'd cooled down enough to compose a telegram to Sir Richard: NOT FOR ANY OTHER MAN WOULD I DO THIS BUT I WILL STEP ASIDE AND MANAGE YOUR CAMPAIGN AS WELL.

The campaign ran so smoothly that Squires won by a landslide, both in Humber and across Newfoundland. Joey hurried off to St. John's, where he waited patiently for Sir Richard to give him an important job in his new administration. When the offer came, it was hardly what Joey had hoped for: justice of the peace. He had learned that the first lesson of politics was to expect deception and betrayal, not good faith and honour.

By now, Clara was caring for a second baby, their son William having just been born. She was alone most of the time and always in need of money. Joey's letters were filled with the urgency of his busy life. One note read: "Clara: Just back in for a few minutes before 6. Just time to enclose all I have on me — $2.00. Sending you flour 1 sk [sack] beans 1 sk rice, 22 lbs butter, 1 sk sugar Tuesday's train."

As the *Herald* grew, Joey became more aware of his wife's needs and more protective of his family. When he decided Clara should bring the children to him on the overnight train, he sent her thirty dollars. "I want you, as soon as you get this, to go or phone the station and reserve the drawing room of the sleeper, it will be $15, perhaps $10 more than a berth. This will mean that you will have absolute privacy and by keeping the door locked there will be no danger to the children. You can have your meals brought in, there will be no need of going out to the dining car."

Joey's new solicitude for Clara and the children would be needed. Newfoundland, along with the rest of the world, was about to plunge into the Great Depression. He could see the handwriting on the wall and disposed of the *Humber Herald* to his remaining partner, who promptly sold it to the *Western Star.* It was then Joey got a call from Sir Richard Squires, now ensconced as premier at the Colonial Building in St. John's. There was a Conservative paper in St. John's, the *Watchman,* that had gone bankrupt, and the Sheriff had put its plant up for sale. Sir Richard gave Joey three thousand dollars to buy the equipment. That was on a Wednesday. By Saturday, Joey's new paper, the *Watchdog,* was being hawked on the streets by the same boys who had sold the *Watchman.* Joey filled it with Liberal propaganda and took great delight in mailing copies to all the Tory subscribers of the old paper. He chuckled with the thought they probably wouldn't notice the new name, but they'd be sure to be puzzled by what they were reading.

As the Depression took hold, the Squires government was powerless to ease the pain of lost markets and declining fishery prices. Public anger played out in several riots. In the 1932 election, Joey was given the Liberal nomination in Fortune Bay. He was beaten badly, along with Squires and all but two other Liberals. A Conservative government took over, but it lasted barely two years. On February 16, 1934, the Newfoundland House of Assembly voted itself out of existence and democracy came to an end in Newfoundland after seventy-eight years as a self-governing colony and three years (since the Statute of Westminster in 1931) as a dominion, equal to Britain. Newfoundland had found itself unable to pay the interest on its debt of nearly one hundred million dollars. London had come to the rescue with a Commission of Government — the governor, Sir David Anderson, plus three Britons and three Newfoundlanders. It put an end to "politics as usual" in Newfoundland and would rule the island in a business-like fashion for the next fifteen years. Ironically, Joey Smallwood had told voters during the election that Newfoundland might as well close down its House of Assembly and petition the king "to appoint a Commission to run the country for the next ten or fifteen years." His memoirs have him telling voters: "It's time to have a long political holiday — both parties have gone intellectually bankrupt."

By now, the *Watchdog* had folded and Joey was again without work. Knowing how horrible conditions had become in the outports, he set out to form a fishermen's co-operative union. It was his idea that fishermen should process and sell their product themselves rather than turn over their catch to avaricious middlemen. He rented a house in Bonavista for eight dollars a month, and brought Clara and the children — now there was a third, Clara, born in 1930 — from Carbonear.

The only way to get to most of the outports was by water, and that meant Joey needed a boat. He borrowed eight hundred dollars from a friend and bought the *Margaret P*, thirty-eight feet of doubtful seaworthiness complete with sail. Now came the hard part: sailing the coast and recruiting members for his union. Joey knew nothing about sailing, and he hired an eighty-year-old retired sea captain, George Mills, and took on another fellow, George Mouland, as engineer, cook, and general cleanup man. The trio sailed the *Margaret P* from Bonavista to St. John's, where Joey had his family down to the dock to see this latest of his exploits.

Joey's brother Reginald, just out of school, had often stood on Signal Hill and watched the boats go out to sea, wishing he could be on one of them. When Joey offered to take him along for the summer, he leapt at the opportunity. He spent his first night aboard the *Margaret P* in the harbor, and at dawn, after a breakfast of boiled salt fish, homemade bread, and partridge-berry jam, they headed out. Joey was still asleep in his bunk. "Joe was reading all night," Reg was told. "Let him sleep." An hour later, with the sail up and the ship rocking in the face of a gathering storm, Joey came on deck. Worried, Reg asked him how they were going to ride out the storm. "What storm?" Joey replied. His brother was never sure whether Joey was joking or just oblivious to danger.

Reg tells the story of that summer on the *Margaret P*:

> We travelled the northeast coast for about two
> months, visiting almost every town. Between

1932 and 1935 Joe enlisted about 8,500
fishermen in the Union. During the summer,
we were asked out to meals. We ate on board.
The meals consisted of some kind of fish. The
fishermen, lacking refrigeration, had no meat
during the summer. In the fall, they killed a
cow, a sheep, or a pig, but there was nothing
wrong with a salmon and a potato or a lobster
dinner. Joey really loved lobster. He could eat it
three times a day — and on some days he did.
He also liked fish and brewis. Actually, I think
he liked just about everything.

In his memoirs, Joey Smallwood writes that his experiences
in the outports, whether they were ones he sailed into in summer
or that he trekked to through snow and ice in winter (as he did
through the hills to get to Keels from Tickle Cove), gained him
"a new knowledge and understanding of Newfoundland …
especially of life in the outports."

Most Newfoundland outports lacked electricity, roads,
medical services, or any form of contact with the outside world
except a radio. Some of the more fortunate had a resident nurse
whose home served as a makeshift hospital, and one or two
church-run elementary schools. Supplies brought in on the last
government steamer in the fall had to last through until the
spring. A doctor might visit once or twice a year. Beriberi was
rampant and tuberculosis was common. Their spray-drenched
houses, built of wood and assembled from whatever other
material might be at hand, went unpainted. Often, the houses
were perched on bare rock and had to be fastened down by ring
bolts and iron cables to prevent their being blown away. Yet the

occupants, from the oldest grannies to the youngest children, were vigorous and venturesome and looked on their lot in life as no more hazardous than any folk.

In the three years that Joey carried his co-operative message to the outports of the northeast coast, he succeeded in winning over the fishermen to the union, but almost nothing came of his efforts. Times were so bad that little or nothing could be accomplished toward improving their conditions. He lacked the money for the five-hundred-dollar-a-year salary he'd promised himself. His main success, a producer-consumer co-operative he established at Pouch Cove, near St. John's, made a bit of money and did manage to last several years.

Joey had always done better for himself in journalism than in union work or politics, and now a new scheme came to mind. He would publish a handsome *Book of Newfoundland*, with articles from various writers on every aspect of the island's life. He coaxed a five thousand dollar investment from a well-known businessman, Chesley Crosbie, son of Sir John Crosbie. Joey took the manuscript and illustrations to England for printing, where he had ten thousand copies of the two-volume set run off. Unfortunately, not many Newfoundlanders had five dollars to spend on such extravagance. Once again, one of Joey's schemes had failed to flourish. But from the *Book of Newfoundland* came a great idea.

Joey went to the *St. John's Daily News* and proposed to write a column on Newfoundland life, drawing on his experiences from the outports and the pulp mill towns. The publisher, John S. Currie, liked the idea and hired Joey at twenty dollars a week. Joey called the column "From the Masthead" and signed it "The Barrelman," seeing himself as a ship's lookout, telling those on deck what he saw on the horizon. After a few weeks, Joey

Smallwood delivering his radio program, The Barrelman, *circa 1937.*

approached St. John's radio station, VONF, with the idea of a nightly broadcast version of the column. When Frank O'Leary, who ran a trading and import company, agreed to sponsor him, Joey dashed off an excited note to Clara: "O'Leary is sponsoring the program starting Monday night. $40 a week out of which I have to pay station $20 or maybe $15. I applied for the five-room furnished flat — no reply yet. Am rushed off my feet."

To the sound effects of a ship's bell, *The Barrelman* went on the air with Joey telling his listeners he was there to "make Newfoundland better known to Newfoundlanders."

He filled his fifteen minutes with tall tales, jokes, and stories of achievements of Newfoundlanders in all walks of life. The program was a sensation. Six nights a week, he spoke to the people of Newfoundland, inviting them to send him their stories, which he repeated on the air. He would end each with the same tag line: "Proving once again, ladies and gentlemen, that Newfoundlanders have what it takes every time they get the chance!" Joey had found his niche. And he had proven to himself that, like other Newfoundlanders, he also had what it takes.

4

Plotting the Scheme

Joey Smallwood, father of three, celebrated broadcaster, writer of note, stood by the side of Kenmount Road, a ragged gravel route that ran along what was then the northern outskirts of St. John's. Scanning the partly forested property in front of him, his eyes settled on the old frame house and a barn of more recent vintage that stood not far from the road. It was September 1939, and these forty acres, bought by Joey at the bargain price of three thousand dollars, were just what he needed to hatch his newest scheme — literally.

Joey's two years of writing and broadcasting as The Barrelman had left him moderately well off. He'd bought a pleasant two-storey house on LeMarchant Road and tooled around the countryside in a second-hand car, looking for stories. Remembering his boyhood days, he always had a desire to get into farming. Clara was uncertain whether she wanted to give up the comforts of their in-town home, but as always, she went along with Joey. She put in a large garden and picked the plentiful crops of berries that grew on the hillside while the children romped through the fields. Soon, Joey had them carrying out small duties in his new venture, chicken farming.

By the end of the winter, Joey had a flock of 1,500 chickens and was selling eggs at the bargain price of a dollar a dozen. With the Second World War on, food prices were rising, and eggs imported from Canada were becoming expensive. One of his best customers was the Newfoundland Hotel, where he went every day to do his broadcasts from the radio station on its top floor. He might have kept on raising chickens indefinitely, but disaster struck his flock. The lack of a steady feed supply forced Joey to give his chickens whatever he could get his hands on. The hens promptly stopped laying. Desperate, he sold his flock, and despite his dislike for fresh pork, decided to try pig farming. He fed them swill, barrels of food remnants from the mess at the U.S. Air Force base at Fort Pepperrell, on the edge of St. John's. That went well until the hogs came down with necrotic enteritis, wiping out most of his herd.

It is likely that Smallwood would have given up farming but for the arrival at Kenmount Road of Group Captain David Anderson of the Royal Air Force. He was in charge of Transport Command at Gander, where a huge air base was being built to serve the British, Canadian, and American air forces that were dispatching planes to Britain and patrolling the Atlantic to defend convoys from German submarines.* Anderson, a colorful character who had survived a

---

* After the war, Gander would become the refuelling stop for pre-jet airliners crossing the Atlantic, continuing later as an important civilian airport. The town would provide refuge to some eight thousand passengers when U.S. flights were diverted there on September 11, 2001, following the attack on the World Trade Centre.

plane crash and married a wealthy American woman, invited Joey to go to Gander and take over the operation of the base piggery. His proposition: a fifty-fifty share with the RAF Welfare Fund of the profits from a herd of perhaps a thousand pigs, all fed on the waste swill from the base. Joey found that Gander, once just a small bush community, had overnight become one of the liveliest towns in Newfoundland, filled with daredevil young men who were determined to have a good time before the fates of wartime flying caught up with them. He saw a profitable business opportunity. With money borrowed from his reliable backer, Ches Crosbie, he oversaw the construction of a new piggery and began to entertain a stream of prominent visitors who passed through Gander, now a sort of crossroads of the world.

The new venture meant the end of Joey's days as The Barrelman. He turned over the broadcast over to a young writer, Michael Harrington, and threw himself completely into raising hogs. It was only at slaughter time that Joey didn't like to be around the piggery. This led the workers there, including Joey's brother Reg, to employ an artful diversion whenever they felt like taking a break to enjoy a shot of whisky, a practice Joey disapproved of during working hours. They'd get out their butchering knives and start sharpening them. Joey would soon disappear, and the boys would enjoy a half-hour break, partaking of liquid refreshment.

While Joey never ate fresh pork, he had no objection to processed pork, and this got him to thinking that instead of selling off surplus hog carcasses the base should be making its own hams, bacon, and chops. He turned again to books and read everything he could on the subject but decided he needed practical advice. Off Joey went to Guelph, Ontario, to learn everything he could from the former superintendent of Canada Packers, Tom Olsen. In a week, Olsen showed Joey how to set up a smoke house and turn out hams, bacon, sausages, and other pork products.

The piggery was making a profit, and Joey had spare time to indulge in other pursuits. He organized three separate unions, hosted debate nights among the workers, and started a consumers' co-op. When the air forces pulled out at the end of the war, he saw to it that their facilities became civilian property; the RCAF library became the Gander Public Library. Joey also managed to get his hands on three thousand surplus army blankets, which he and a partner, Tony Mullowney, bought for three thousand dollars — again, with help from Ches Crosbie — and sold to the Bowaters lumber camps for twice the price. "Any time you want a bit of profitable trading done, call on me," Joey would recall telling Crosbie.

Joey's days in farming made him realize how much Newfoundland lacked in all that was needed to be more self-sufficient, especially when it came to food. Practically everything except fish had to be imported — an expensive and often unreliable practice. In December 1945, Joey hitched a ride on one of the few RAF Transport Command planes still flying between Gander and Montreal. From there he took a train to Toronto, where he met with people in the livestock feed trade, since he was thinking of opening a feed mill in Newfoundland. His business done, he took the overnight train back to Montreal, checked into the Ford Hotel on Dorchester Street (today Rene Lévesque Blvd.), picked up a newspaper, and went into the dining room for breakfast. He placed his order with the waitress and then opened his copy of the *Montreal Gazette*. What he was about to read would change his life.

Joey Smallwood was a few days from his forty-fifth birthday. After years of financial failure, journalistic adventures, and small successes, he'd at last become a man of property with the place on Kenmount Road and a half-share in what had been a profitable piggery in Gander, where he was now living full-time. But he was not wealthy by any means, and with his family growing up he had to make sure he could continue to support them and, as he earnestly wished, send his children to university. That was why he'd gone to Toronto to investigate feed mills: he knew business at the piggery would dry up once the last of the airmen left Gander.

Turning to the newspaper before him, Joey read what for him was earth-shaking news. SELF-RULE IS PLAN FOR NEWFOUNDLAND, the headline told him. The headline didn't have it quite right, but after twenty years of unelected commission government, Newfoundland was to be given a chance to decide its democratic future. Britain's new Labour government of Clement Atlee had announced that Newfoundlanders would be given the opportunity to elect members to the National Convention. Its task would be to study the country's economic condition and recommend possible future forms of government. The choices would be put to the voters in a referendum; if there were more than two and no choice received a majority, a second referendum would decide between the two with the most votes.

Joey's appetite suddenly deserted him. He raced through the story, then read it over again, more carefully. This was what he had wondered about for years. How was Newfoundland ever to regain self-rule? This decision put it in the hands of the people. All of Joey's old dream of a life in politics, maybe even becoming the prime minister of Newfoundland, rose again in his mind. He was going to be in it, he told himself. All the king's horses and all the king's men couldn't keep him out of it. But what scheme would be the best for Newfoundland? What side would he come down on? Certainly not on the side of more commission government. He knew the perils of responsible government and the mess that irresponsible politicians had made of things in the past. And he remembered the words of an old friend, Gordon Bradley, one of the few Newfoundland politicians that Joey respected: "Mark my words," he had told Joey on one of their many walks around Quidi Vidi Lake, "Confederation with Canada is our only hope, our only salvation!"

Joey spent the day wandering the streets of Montreal, thinking about what he should do. Late that afternoon, he decided to phone an old Newfoundland friend, Ewart Young, who ran a small monthly magazine, the *Atlantic Guardian*, from his Montreal apartment. Young invited him over, and when Joey arrived, proofs of the next issue lay about. The magazine was usually filled with articles like one Young had just edited, "Where the Cod is King," telling readers that "from a single codfish the thrifty Newfoundland housewife can serve up a dozen different delicacies." Joey helped Young put together a story he'd been asked to write for the next day's *Christian Science Monitor*, published in Boston. "London's decision to restore responsible government to Britain's oldest colony has delighted most Newfoundlanders but finds them almost totally unprepared to meet its implications," they wrote. Perhaps Joey was reflecting his own uncertainty. They talked until 3:00 a.m., by which time Young had given Joey a thorough indoctrination in the mysteries of Canada's federal system, based on what he'd learned living in the country's largest city. By the time Joey Smallwood left Young's apartment, he was a convinced advocate of Confederation.

Joey slept until noon in his room at the Ford Hotel, when he awoke with a start. All that he had talked and thought about with Ewart Young tumbled through his mind. Dressing quickly, he hurried to the airport and was able to catch an RAF bomber that was returning to Gander that night. Clara and the children were asleep when he got home. He lay awake for a long time considering his next step. It was then he realized he needed to know more about Canada if he was to be an effective advocate — and a winning candidate — on the side of Confederation.

The next morning, after finishing a quick breakfast, Joey pushed aside a pile of papers and magazines on the table where he worked and put paper in his typewriter. He wrote ten letters, one to the prime minister of Canada and to each of the nine provincial premiers. He told them he had decided to offer himself as a candidate for election to the National Convention: "I wish to make a careful study of what effect would be had upon Newfoundland and her people if Newfoundland were to become a Province of Canada. Would you be kind enough to assist me in this study?" Joey asked to receive budget speeches, annual reports, or anything "that would throw light on the subject."

While he waited to hear back, Joey worried about where he would get the money to finance his campaign. The rules laid down by London required that a candidate for the National Convention run in the place where they were "ordinarily resident." That meant Joey would stand for the district of Bonavista Centre which included Gander. He had next to no money. The fifteen hundred dollars he had earned from the blanket caper — what was left after giving Ches Crosbie and his partner, Tom Mullowney, their cuts — had gone to pay off debts. What rescued him was Tom's decision to give his share to Joey for the campaign. "Take it, Joey," he said, "and get yourself elected."

Joey Smallwood knew very well that his fellow Newfoundlanders possessed little understanding of the democratic process. The only elections in Newfoundland in the past decade had been for the local council in St. John's, where no one but property owners had voted. And most people, Joey also realized, knew almost nothing of Canada. He would have to educate them on both counts.

On March 1, 1946, Joey launched his scheme for Confederation — the most daring scheme of his life. He'd had answers to all his letters and he'd made a thorough study of the mountain of material he'd received. He decided to make use of all this information by writing a series of eleven articles in which he explained how the Canadian system of Confederation worked, and the benefits to be gained if Newfoundland were a part of it. He took the articles to John S. Currie, publisher of the *Daily News*, who agreed to run them as letters to the editor. A friend of Joey's but also an anti-Confederate, Currie didn't want it to look as if he were favouring that side. The letters established Joey as an authority on Canada, and he built on that reputation with speeches to various groups throughout his district. At first, he would speak for three to four hours, often using a blackboard to explain his points. Uncertain as how to best describe Confederation, he hit on the idea of relating it to the way individual lodges or fraternal societies — to which many Newfoundlanders belonged — were part of larger organizations. The lodges looked after their local affairs, and the larger organization acted on common, broader matters. In the same way, Joey explained, provinces ran their own affairs and the central government at Ottawa acted on national matters like defence, external relations, income tax, and so on.

All that spring, Joey canvassed his district, growing ever more confident he would be elected, despite the drunks and antagonists at his meetings. "Don't vote for me," he would tell his listeners, "unless you want to be represented by a man who will fight to get Canada's terms and conditions of Confederation." One day, as he alighted from a freight train that had brought him close to the coastal settlement of Glovertown, Joey noticed that sparks from the engine had started a grass fire. An hour later, as Joey canvassed door to door for support, the fire had grown to raging proportions and was threatening the village. He began to urge people to evacuate their homes and get down to the water's edge. In the next few hours, most of the outport was wiped out, with more than seventy houses, shops and other buildings burned to the ground. Joey put some burned-out families aboard a boat he'd chartered and caught a train to St. John's. There, he went on the air to appeal for funds to help the destitute settlement.

If Confederation was to receive a thumping endorsement in Bonavista Centre, Joey knew, it was essential that an opponent run against him! If he were elected by acclamation, that would be no victory for his Confederation scheme. He had heard that one other man, Kitchener Pritchett, intended to contest the election. Joey would later admit in his memoirs that as the election neared and no opposing candidate had come forward, "strenuous efforts" (the nature of which have never been explained) had to be exerted to ensure Pritchett's nomination. On election day, June 21, Joey won his required landslide victory — 2,129 votes to 277 for Pritchett. Confederation, as Joey saw it, had been endorsed by 89 percent of the voters.

The National Convention was due to open in September and Joey knew it would be at work for months, if not years. He decided it was time to cash in on everything he'd worked for and sell his interest in the Gander piggery, as well as the farm on Kenmount Road. He came away from the piggery with six thousand dollars as his share, but it was what he got for the farm that eased all of his financial worries. St. John's was growing and property was much in demand. In addition to the three thousand dollars Joey had paid for the forty acres back in 1939, he'd put in a thousand dollars on improvements and had spent two thousand dollars on a new bungalow — a total of six thousand dollars. He got one hundred and twenty-five thousand dollars, free and clear of taxes.

But before the Convention opened, Joey decided, he would go to Ottawa for a personal talk with Prime Minister Mackenzie King. He sent word he was coming, and when he got there he found appointments had been made for him with various departments of government, such as agriculture, public works, and fisheries. That was fine, but Joey wanted to see the top man. Learning that Mackenzie King was away, he began to hang around the parliament buildings in hopes of seeing the acting prime minister, Louis St. Laurent.

One day, as he loitered at the entrance to a small office used by the prime minister just behind the Speaker's chair in the House of Commons, Joey encountered Mr. King's chief assistant, Jack Pickersgill. When Pickersgill heard the visitor's name, he recognized it. Joey Smallwood, he knew, had been the only publicly declared supporter of Confederation elected to Newfoundland's National Convention. He explained to Joey that Mr. St. Laurent would be in the House for a while, but that in the meantime, he would be glad to talk to him. After an hour's discussion, Pickersgill would remember that he "required no convincing that Canada needed Newfoundland." Joey spent fifteen minutes with Mr. St. Laurent and left with the feeling Canada would not deny Newfoundland a chance to enter Confederation. He remembered Mr. King's cautious words back in 1943, when he'd been asked about it. "If the people of Newfoundland should ever decide that they wish to enter the Canadian federation," King had said, "and should they make that decision clear beyond all possibility of misunderstanding, Canada would give most sympathetic consideration to the proposal." It was as bold a come-on, Joey thought, as Canada would ever likely give. He'd have to make sure Ottawa would have no reason to say no.

5

Confederates Together

Ever since his return to Newfoundland in 1925, Joey Smallwood had shown an uncanny ability to be present for great events that would shake the island — both literally and figuratively. He was in Newfoundland when a 7.2-magnitude earthquake rattled the eastern shore of the Burin Peninsula on November 18, 1929, setting off a tsunami that devastated outports, took at least twenty-eight lives, and disrupted fishing stocks. Later, during a night in April 1932, he was barricaded in the Colonial Building with the last Liberal prime minister, Sir Richard Squires, while an angry mob of ten thousand descended on it, demanding relief and jobs. Too old to enlist in the Second World War, Smallwood was on hand at Gander when thousands of Allied servicemen were posted there, needing food that his piggery would help supply. And now, on September 11, 1946, he was present as the representative for Bonavista Centre when Newfoundland's last colonial governor, Sir Gordon Macdonald, swore in the forty-five members of the National Convention.

The swearing-in was a great social as well as political occasion. Everyone who was anyone in St. John's — the Crosbies, the Bowerings, the Cashins, and the Herders, along with commission officials and representatives of the United Kingdom, Canada, and the military — attended the swearing in and the receptions that followed. The drafty old Colonial Building, where members of the House of Assembly had met in years past, had been scrubbed, dusted, and its insides given a new coat of paint. Erected in 1850 and clad still in its original facing of white limestone brought from Ireland, flanked by six massive porticos, the old building once again dominated Military Road. The Lower Chamber, the former home of the Assembly, had been emptied of the temporary offices put in by the commission government. It was now to be the scene of ferocious debate as Newfoundlanders argued over the shape of their future.

Amid the smiles and gaiety, Joey Smallwood felt gripped by the tension of this historic occasion. His wife Clara and their daughter, also named Clara, stood at his side as he received the congratulations (not always heartfelt, Joey thought) of his fellow members. In the days leading up to the Convention, Joey had haunted the Newfoundland Railway train terminal, meeting delegates as they came in from their rural districts. It was like the old days on the docks in Brooklyn when he'd greeted arrivals on the Red Cross liners. He was criticized for his shameless canvassing of the National Convention members, but he was determined to get on a first-name basis with every one. Joey also wanted to measure their support for Confederation. By opening day, he was able to come up with only a slim list of supporters — perhaps a third of the members at most. He dared not share the numbers with even his most ardent supporter, Gordon Bradley. The old judge and onetime leader of the Liberal Party would have been aghast at the long odds. "Confederation with Canada is our only hope, our only salvation," he had told Joey.

It was time to give it his all. Smallwood moved into a room in the Newfoundland Hotel, leaving his family in their newly rented brick townhouse on Devon Row. The Convention sat from three to six o'clock every afternoon, Monday to Friday, and those three hours of debate were recorded on wax discs and broadcast every night on the Newfoundland government radio station. It was a break beyond anything for which Joey Smallwood could have dreamt. The debates captured the imagination of Newfoundlanders, and in outports where radios were few, people gathered in the homes of neighbours after supper to listen. Of all the voices they heard, none rang with such fervor or familiarity as that of the old Barrelman, Joey Smallwood.

The debates left ample time for the work of ten committees appointed to examine every aspect of Newfoundland life, and Joey served on the committees for education, health, and welfare. He was interested in all these subjects, but he poured most of his energy into preparing the speech in which he'd ask the Convention to a send a delegation to Ottawa to discuss terms of Confederation. He knew the delegates were far from ready to throw in their lot with Canada, and so he couched his motion carefully, noting that "the delegation should have no authority whatsoever to negotiate or conclude any agreement." It would be simply a fact-finding mission.

On October 27, when Joey rose to speak to his motion, his wife and daughter sat spellbound. Daughter Clara, unaccountably, found herself seated next to the sergeant-at-arms. Looking around, Smallwood began with a tribute to the past: "Our people's struggle to live commenced on the day that they first landed here, four centuries and more ago, and has continued to this day. Their struggle is more uneven now than it was then, and the people view the future now with more dread than they felt a century ago." The sombre beginning, however, soon gave way to a brutally frank, even cruel, indictment of Newfoundland life and the island's failure to keep pace with the rest of the world. As he spoke, delegates stirred uneasily in their seats, embarrassed, angry, or distraught at Joey Smallwood's litany of Newfoundland's problems:

> We have been taught by newspapers, magazines, motion pictures, radios and visitors something of the higher standards of well-being of the mainland of North America; we have become uncomfortably aware of the low standards of our country; and we are driven irresistibly to wonder whether our attempt to persist in isolation is the root-cause of our condition. We have often felt in the past, when we learned something of the higher standards of the mainland, that such things belonged to another world, that they were not for us ... Today we are not so sure, not so ready to take it for granted, that we Newfoundlanders are destined to accept much lower standards of life than our neighbours ...
>
> Compared with the mainland of North America, we are fifty years, in some things a hundred years, behind the times. We live more poorly, more shabbily, mire meanly. Our life is more a struggle. Our struggle is tougher, more naked, more hopeless. In the North American family, Newfoundland bears the reputation of

having the lowest standards of life, of being the least progressive and advanced, of the whole family ...

We have grown up in such an atmosphere of struggle, of adversity, of mean times that we are never surprised, never shocked, when we learn that we have one of the highest rates of tuberculosis in the world; one of the highest infant mortality rates in the world; one of the highest rates of beriberi and rickets in the world. We take these shocking facts for granted. We take for granted our lower standards, our poverty. We are not indignant about them. We save our indignation for those who publish such facts, for with all our complacency, with all our readiness to receive, to take for granted, and even to justify these things amongst ourselves, we are strange to say, angry and hurt when these shocking facts become known to the outside world ...

Our danger, or so it seems to me, is that of nursing delusions of grandeur ... We are not a nation. We are merely a medium-size municipality, a mere miniature borough of a large city ... There was a time when tiny states lived gloriously. That time is now ancient European history ...

By now, catcalls and boos were being heard throughout the Chamber. Never had there been such a display of disloyalty in a Newfoundland public forum. The delegates hung on his closing words:

> Confederation I will support if it means a lower cost of living for our people. Confederation I will support if it means a higher standard of life for our people. Confederation I will support if it means strength, stability, and security for Newfoundland ... I believe with all my heart and mind that the people will bless the day this resolution was moved. With God's grace, let us move forward for a brighter and happier Newfoundland.

There was little blessing for Joey Smallwood that night at the National Convention, or in the days to follow before his resolution was put to a vote on Tuesday, November 5. Smallwood's old colleague Michael Harrington, to whom he had turned over the Barrelman radio show and who had been elected a delegate, claimed Joey had tried to bribe him with the promise of a seat in the Canadian Senate. Peter Cashin, a strident advocate for a return to responsible government, called Smallwood a Judas Iscariot and a Quisling (after the Norwegian traitor who sold out his country to the Nazis in the Second World War). The vote was twenty-five in opposition to sending a delegation to Ottawa, only eighteen in support. Many thought the outcome sounded the death knell for Confederation, but Joey Smallwood was not deterred; he knew the weeklong debate had given him the chance to air its benefits to thousands of listeners. Confederation had become the issue that would not die.

One reason Confederation would not die was that neither

London nor Ottawa were prepared to allow it to expire. The governor of Newfoundland, Sir Gordon Macdonald, was a close friend of British prime minister Clement Attlee. Britain was struggling to recover from the devastation of the war, and Atlee made it clear it had no money to throw away on its long-time colony. Macdonald subverted an attempt by the Convention to send a delegation to Washington to discuss union with the U.S. No way, he told the delegates — overtures to the Americans were beyond their mandate. On March 1, 1947, the Convention agreed at last to send two delegations: one to London and the other to Ottawa. Gordon Bradley headed the London mission, but he was almost the only one of its seven members who supported Confederation. The others, especially Peter Cashin and Ches Crosbie, remained strong advocates of responsible government. The hopes of the London delegation were dashed when London advised them that financial support and responsible government could not co-exist; the two just didn't mix.

In contrast, the Ottawa delegation, which set out after the return of the London mission, found a warm welcome, both politically and in the weather in the Canadian capital. Gordon Bradley also headed that mission. Clad in tweed suits and woolen underwear suitable for the cool Newfoundland climate, he suffered from an oppressive Ottawa heat wave, even after Smallwood convinced him to buy a linen suit and boxer shorts. Discussions in Ottawa dragged on, partly because Smallwood felt delaying would help turn the tide for Confederation. When the delegation finally returned to St. John's, it came not with terms of union, but a set of "Black Books," in which the Canadian government described how the federal system worked and what Ottawa did for the provinces.

Smallwood at the first meeting in Ottawa in 1947, with Prime Minister Mackenzie King and Louis St. Laurent.

The content of the Black Books, setting out the aid provinces receive from Ottawa, along with a letter from Mackenzie King, were conveyed in a motion by Gordon Bradley to the Convention on November 6, 1947. First, however, it had to dispose of an economic report submitted by Peter Cashin on behalf of the finance committee. It argued that Newfoundland had again become solvent, thus justifying a return to responsible government. When the Convention got around to Bradley's motion, he had fallen ill and it was left to Smallwood to make the argument for Confederation. Debate raged until Christmas and started up again on January 5, 1948, going on for another ten days.

To Joey Smallwood, those weeks were a glorious opportunity to extol the benefits of union with Canada. They were also days when emotions ran high. On one occasion, Joey got into a shouting match with Peter Cashin during a meeting of the Convention's steering committee. Before anyone realized

Smallwood speaking to the National Convention about the future of Newfoundland and its people.

what was happening, the two were wrestling on the floor. Joey claimed Cashin had rushed at him and had hit in the face. Once separated, Joey declared, "I'll show you how scared I am of you!" He lit a cigarette and blew smoke in Cashin's face.

On January 15, the Convention finally agreed that the terms from Ottawa would be put into the record. It then turned to considering the forms of government that Newfoundlanders would vote on. A motion that the ballot include responsible government and the commission form of government passed easily, on the understanding this did not preclude consideration of other forms of government.

The next day, Smallwood went before the Convention with a motion for Confederation to be added to the ballot. Perhaps letting on more than he should, he predicted Newfoundlanders would have the opportunity to vote for Confederation even if his motion was defeated by "a mere majority of this convention." He then made a savage, albeit eloquent, attack on Newfoundland's establishment of merchants, bankers, and resource companies. The opponents of Confederation, he charged, were led by parasitic monopolists who represented "a new race of traders [which] has arisen in our midst." The country was being run by "twenty millionaires along Water Street" and it was time to put a stop to their depredations. Another two-week debate, capped by an all-night session on January 27, ended shortly after five o'clock in the morning on the 28th. Smallwood's motion, like those before, was convincingly defeated, 29 to 16.

The National Convention dissolved the next day, but the furor over Smallwood's speech had barely begun. Bradley went on the air with a speech written for him by Smallwood denouncing "the twenty-nine dictators" for denying Newfoundlanders the right to vote for, or even against, Confederation. In less than a week Smallwood received thousands of telegrams as well as petitions signed by almost fifty thousand people, demanding Confederation be put on the ballot. He took every last one of them to Governor Macdonald and asked that they be forwarded to London. The governor never actually sent the telegrams and petitions, but he did file a lengthy report describing them. On March 10, word finally came from London. The Newfoundland Broadcasting Corporation dispatched its newscaster, Dick O'Brien, to Government House to pick up the official announcement. Standing in the corridor outside the radio studio at the Newfoundland Hotel, Joey Smallwood waited nervously for his return. A broad wink from O'Brien sent Joey's spirits soaring. A few moments later, all Newfoundland got the news: His Majesty's government was of the view that Confederation, as well as the commission form of government and responsible government, should appear on the referendum ballot. Newfoundlanders would have their say!

The referendum was set for June 3, 1948, less than three months away. If Joey Smallwood's great scheme for Confederation was to win, an equally great campaign would have to be mounted. It would need money, volunteers, and an effective publicity machine. To cut expenses, Joey moved out of the Newfoundland Hotel, retreating to his townhouse, where Clara and the children awaited him. Clara told him it was time to clean up his bedraggled appearance, and Joey invested in several double-breasted suits, a collection of white shirts, and a selection of colorful bow ties. He set up a campaign office in a back room at Bartlett's barber shop on Water Street and on March 26 filled the ballroom of the Newfoundland Hotel with a rally launching the Confederate Association.

Joey needed a loyal team alongside him. He chose well, picking Harold Horwood, a St. John's journalist; Greg Power, who'd run for the National Convention but had failed to get elected; and Philip Forsey, an old friend. Dozens of others pitched in. Gordon Bradley took on the role of president, but it was Joey, as campaign manager, who called the shots. "I was the leader," Joey would recall, admitting he had been practically a "dictator" — at least "a conductor with more than the usual authority over the orchestra."

The campaign office was filled with volunteers, but the real decisions were made late at night back at Joey's townhouse, where his team gathered around a cluttered dining room table while Clara retreated to the kitchen, possibly to escape the presence of Harold Horwood, who seldom bothered to bathe at that time in his life. Philip Forsey guaranteed a bank loan to finance the first issue of a weekly paper, the *Confederate*. The loan was repaid with donations from across Canada, much of the money coming from corporations who were regular donors to the Liberal Party of Canada. Promises of Senate seats were sold off at a thousand dollars a crack.

Fifty thousand copies of the *Confederate* were run off every week, singing the glories of Canadian family allowances, higher pensions, and the lower food prices that Confederation would bring. Every issue featured a cutting cartoon by Canada's leading cartoonist, Jack Booth of the Toronto *Globe and Mail*. Joey dreamt up the ideas, sketched them in rough form, and sent them on to Booth.

Joey took to the airwaves and addressed dozens of public meetings. But it was his flight around Newfoundland in a tiny one-engine float plane that caught the attention of outport voters. The plane would swoop into an outport harbour and Joey, armed with a loudspeaker, would clamber onto a pontoon to address people gathered on shore. Sometimes, welcoming parties fired off volleys of shotgun blasts to announce his arrival.

The anti-Confederates, made up largely of Newfoundland's upper economic strata, split their forces between responsible government and a return to commission government. A wild card came into play when the young and aggressive publisher of the *Sunday Herald*, Geoff Stirling, with the support of Joey's old financial backer, Ches Crosbie, launched the Economic Union Party. Its aim: union with the United States. That option wasn't on the ballot, forcing the Unionists to urge a return to responsible government. As a dominion, they argued, Newfoundland could then negotiate its way into the States. Joey and his Confederate team ridiculed the idea, but it worried him enough that he offered a deal to Crosbie: switch sides, and he could have the premiership. Crosbie declined.

The referendum of June 3 failed to settle the island's fate; none of the three choices on the ballot gained a majority:

Responsible Government	69,400
Confederation	64,006
Commission of Government	22,311

A second referendum was ordered, for July 22, with Confederation and responsible government the only options. Compared to the first campaign, this would become a nasty affair, burdened with religious prejudice and regional hostility, pitting Catholics against Protestants and city against the outports. In the main, Catholic church leaders strongly opposed Confederation. The Archbishop of Newfoundland, Edward Patrick Roche, feared that "a simple God-fearing way of life" would be contaminated by the Protestant morality of modern Canada, leading to divorce and mixed marriages.

Both sides calculated that the second vote would turn on the 22,000 ballots cast for commission government. This meant paying more attention to St. John's, and Joey Smallwood campaigned continuously in the capital, while also managing to make fifty-six speeches in fifty-six outports over the space of two days. At his main St. John's rally, a mob of anti-Confederates forced their way into the meeting, ready to assault Smallwood on his exit. Protected by two bodyguards, he fled through a side door and took refuge in a small out-of-town hotel.

Thursday, July 22, 1948, dawned as a typically cool Newfoundland summer day. The voting was even more orderly, if that was possible, than it had been seven weeks earlier. Joey worried that fewer votes were being cast; the offshore fishing season had opened and some ten thousand fishermen were out on the Grand Banks. He also worried about the Catholic vote, but knew little could be done about it. That night, the returns from St. John's once again favoured responsible government. But as the votes were tallied in the country villages and outports, a slim majority for Confederation began to show itself. The outcome would be confirmed the next morning when the last of the ballot boxes was opened:

Confederation	78,323
Responsible Government	71,334

Confederates cheered, but opponents mourned the outcome. Smallwood and his supporters celebrated at a rowdy picnic in a meadow outside Spaniard's Bay, a village fifty miles from St. John's. Anti-Confederates lowered the Union Jack to half mast, wept, and got drunk. Once sober, they plotted ways to stave off union with Canada. The Responsible Government League declared the referendum illegal and asked that its results be set aside. A court case challenging the outcome lost in both the Newfoundland Supreme Court and at the Privy Council in London. Peter Cashin, the most effective opponent of Confederation, collected fifty thousand signatures to a petition he took to London. It did no good.

Smallwood sitting with Mackenzie King at the Liberal leadership convention in August 1948.

In Ottawa, the ever-cautious Mackenzie King wondered whether the margin for Confederation — 52.24 percent — had been sufficiently decisive. His aide, Jack Pickersgill, told him the result was wonderful. "Do you realize that this is a larger majority than you received in any election except 1940?" Convinced, King replied, "That puts a different light on the whole situation."

All through that summer of 1948, Joey Smallwood held Newfoundland in the palm of his hand. He'd stormed the citadels of Water Street, written thousands of words for the *Confederate*, delivered hundreds of speeches across the island, and blunted the attacks of religious bigots who had plastered walls with posters reading CONFEDERATION MEANS FRENCH-CANADIAN UNION. He'd overcome the deeply rooted sectarianism of an island where churches, Protestant as well as Catholic, had run their own school systems for generations, splitting their communities into divisive, distrustful encampments of intolerance. Now all of that was to be consigned to history — a new chapter beckoned in the long and colorful history of Newfoundland.

Years later, Joey Smallwood would recall his happiness over their "glorious victory." He had known he would face insuperable obstacles, but he had "not accepted them as insuperable." The scheme had been won. Now it was time to fulfill the dream.

6

Living the Dream

All his life, Joey Smallwood had been convinced of two things: that he would one day be prime minister of Newfoundland and that he would always be a Socialist. These convictions converged at 11 o'clock on the morning of Friday, April 1, 1949, when he was sworn in as head of the government for Newfoundland and Labrador. The difference in title — he was to be premier rather than prime minister — was but a technicality, reflecting Newfoundland's new status as a Canadian province. As for his Socialist bent, it was of the old school Socialism, a zeal for reform and social and economic justice that he would cling to until his dying day. He chose the Liberal Party as his political vehicle, because its roots ran deep in the fishing and working classes of the island, and because he knew its policies were as close to Socialism as Newfoundlanders would ever accept. His pursuit of these ideals would carry him to the heights of success and acclaim. When he neglected or forgot them, he'd be buffeted onto the rocks by a political nor'wester.

On that raw April day, more wintry than spring, Joey Smallwood and his chosen Cabinet of nine ministers trooped into Government House for the official swearing in, conducted by the new lieutenant governor, Sir Albert Walsh. The choice of Walsh, a lawyer who had been deputy chair of the commission government, was the only key appointment that did not bear Smallwood's personal stamp of approval. He'd wanted Sir Leonard Outerbridge, one of the St. John's elite whom he had cajoled into breaking with his establishment friends and endorsing Confederation in the referendum. A diplomatic dance between Ottawa and St. John's had gone awry when Outerbridge apparently hesitated on the matter of who would be premier. It was all a misunderstanding, but Louis St. Laurent, Mackenzie King's replacement as prime minister, wasn't taking any chances. The premiership had been promised to Joey Smallwood, and the premiership he would get. Walsh was totally agreeable, but he served only a few months as the king's representative before resigning to go to the Newfoundland Supreme Court. Outerbridge succeeded him.

The night before the swearing in, Newfoundland had officially become part of Canada a few moments before the stroke of midnight. On Friday morning, St. Laurent and his Cabinet took to a reviewing stand in front of the parliament buildings in Ottawa for a march past the armed forces. Standing close to the prime minister was Smallwood's old ally Gordon Bradley, who was going into the federal Cabinet as Newfoundland's representative. St. Laurent made him secretary of state, heeding Smallwood's advice that Newfoundland, accustomed to hearing that title attached to one of the most important positions in the U.S, government, would see it as apt recognition for their

Albert Walsh and Prime Minister St. Laurent adding their signatures to the Terms of Union on December 11, 1948. Smallwood is second from the right.

province. "We are all Canadians now," Bradley said, his words going on the CBC radio network to be heard in St. John's over CBN, the new call letters for what had been radio station VONF. Meanwhile, Smallwood presided at a short news conference at Government House, paying tribute to "this proud Canada of which Newfoundland now forms a part."

The road to Confederation had been long and arduous, and even the months after the referendum were filled with doubt and apprehension. The Canadian government formally invited a delegation to come from St. John's to discuss terms of union. Headed by Sir Albert Walsh, with Smallwood as a member, it arrived in Ottawa on October 6, 1948. By December 11, the two sides had reached agreement, and the terms were signed at noon in the Senate Chamber. The only holdout was Joey's old financial backer, Ches Crosbie, who insisted the terms did not make Newfoundland financially secure.

The key to the talks was settling on a grant formula for Newfoundland. Both sides recognized that a massive infusion of money would be needed to bring the island's services up to Canadian standards. Transitional grants were set at forty-seven million dollars, to be paid over twelve years. After that, Newfoundland would benefit from annual transfers from Ottawa in accordance with Term 29 of the Terms of Union. Pension payments would be moved up to Canadian levels, and Canada guaranteed that ferry and coastal freight services would be maintained at current levels. Confederation would bring a billion-dollar-a-year windfall to Joey Smallwood's government.

All was not work and worry for Joey Smallwood in those months leading up to Newfoundland's admission to Confederation. He was no longer campaigning — either for a seat on the National Convention or in the two referendums — and except for the mission to Ottawa in the fall of 1948, he had time to get to know his family again. His two oldest boys — Ramsay, by then a strapping young man of twenty-two, and Bill, twenty — were about to set out on careers of their own. Daughter Clara, nineteen, was a constant companion to her mother when not out riding, which became her favourite pastime. She even rode a horse to school, leaving it tied in the yard during classes. The family usually ate supper together, but after the dishes were cleared away, Joey's strategists began to arrive, one by one, and they'd talk until after midnight, just as they had during the referendums. Harold Horwood would never forget the night that Joey paced the floor of the Devon Row flat, declaring, "I am becoming a national figure." Philip Forsey, standing behind Joey, propped his thumbs into his vest, stuck out his chest, and marched back and forth repeating the words, "A *national figure.*" They all roared with laughter.

It was a rare moment of respite. The new premier's first tasks were to set up an office in the Colonial Building and assemble and train a Cabinet made up of men who had never served in the House of Assembly and who had not yet been elected to any office. They would serve at the pleasure of the lieutenant governor until an election could be held. Many of Joey's preferred choices turned him down, but he was finally able to gather together nine supporters who would make up what Smallwood jocularly referred to as "His Majesty's Outport government." In fact, only three were from outside St. John's, and none from an outport.

From his inner circle, he chose Philip Forsey to be minister of Home Affairs. Horwood agreed to run for a Labrador seat whenever the election was held but did not get a place in the Cabinet. Only one Catholic, William Keough, a union organizer, went to the Cabinet table, as minister of Natural Resources. There was one lawyer, Leslie Curtis, as attorney general. It was clearly a left-leaning Cabinet, but according to Horwood, "the idea of a true democratic government ... was wholly foreign to [Joey's] experience." This may be explained in part by the fact that Smallwood had to train his neophyte ministers to share responsibility for all government decisions as well as handle the affairs of their own departments. When one minister rose to leave a Cabinet meeting after the matters affecting his department had been dealt with, Joey stopped him short. "Your business isn't finished," he'd recall telling him. "Each of you is responsible for everything that Cabinet decides, and each of you will support everything that Cabinet has decided." He was explaining the principles of Cabinet solidarity as practised in the British parliamentary system.

Debate would rage about Smallwood's management of his Cabinet and his relationships with the fifty-odd men who would serve under him over his twenty-three years as premier. Horwood would resign his seat in his first term, join the *Evening Telegram*, and become one of the premier's most bitter critics. He'd claim Smallwood ran a "one-man show" and that "rarely, if ever, was there a formal vote on any issue" in either Cabinet or caucus. Two ministers who served under Smallwood in the 1960s but resigned on matters of principle decried his management style. John Crosbie, for a time Smallwood's minister of municipal affairs before crossing the floor to the Progressive Conservatives, termed him "an absolute monarch" who "treated his cabinet ministers with contempt." According to Clyde Wells, a future premier who quit the Cabinet at the same time, "his style was top down all the way, equals never applied. It was his way in everything." Yet Edward Roberts, who served as Joey's executive assistant and would become leader of the Newfoundland Liberal Party, disagrees with this assessment. "He didn't interfere with cabinet ministers," Roberts recalls, "but if you had something major he'd expect you to come forward. He didn't want to hear about it (for the first time) in the cabinet room." Yet there is no doubt Smallwood's influence was so enormous, and his power so far-reaching, that anyone who crossed him on almost anything he cared about suffered the consequences. Smallwood would denounce Crosbie as "a political tragedy ... just a bagful of hate ... (with) a diseased mind." Horwood he saw as a "dastardly clown, this loathsome literary scavenger, this cut-throat, this rat" who hated him "like the devil hates Holy Water."

Aside from assembling his Cabinet, Joey Smallwood had myriad issues to deal with in his first year as premier. How many of Newfoundland's three hundred thousand people would rush off to Canada now that immigration barriers had been removed? If thousands of young Newfoundlanders couldn't find good jobs, how could they be expected to stay? How rapidly would the federal government staff its offices in Newfoundland to oversee the delivery of family allowances, unemployment insurance, and enriched veterans' and old age pensions? Most important of all, how much financial assistance could Newfoundland count on to build the infrastructure and launch the new projects that it desperately needed to become a modern society?

In fact, money was pouring into the province. Smallwood's government inherited a cash surplus of forty-five million dollars from the old commission government. Joey had plans for a new provincial sales tax of 3 percent, as well as other levies that Newfoundland could employ to raise revenues. Then there was all that federal money. It would be used, Joey had decided, not just for better roads, schools, and hospitals but to jump-start an industrial revolution. Natural resources the province had aplenty, but nobody had any real idea of how much, or even where. A survey was needed.

When Joey Smallwood called the first provincial election for May 27, 1949, he had complete control of his government and his party. He personally handpicked candidates for all twenty-eight seats. In a manifesto titled "Ahead — or Astern," Smallwood made clear his vision for Newfoundland:

> As a Province of Canada, Newfoundland will be either a glorified "poor house" with most of her people depending too largely on Family Allowances, Old Age Pensions and other cash payments from the Government of Canada; or else a growing prosperous Province of independent families. We will either be a drag on the rest of Canada, or we will stand on our own feet as a prosperous, progressive Province.

> The policy of the Liberal Party is to make Newfoundland one of the most prosperous, progressive Provinces of Canada; a Province able to hold its head up and proud to look the rest of Canada squarely in the eyes.
>
> We must find out what natural resources we have in our country; we must advertise these resources throughout the world; we must bring new capital to open up our country and give jobs for our people. Our country will stand or fall according to how far we go to develop our natural resources.

Smallwood was appealing to both the reason and emotion of Newfoundlanders, as the province's natural resources had to be developed. But he also used the designations of "province" and "country" interchangeably, signalling that those who voted against Confederation still had a stake in Newfoundland. The voters agreed and on election day filled twenty-two of the twenty-eight seats with Smallwood's Liberal candidates.

When the House of Assembly met in the Colonial Building, members heard a long list of legislation in the speech from the throne. The focus was on new public services: financial aid for co-operatives and the fisheries, a department of economic development, commissions for public utilities and hydro, a workman's compensation act, and a slum clearance bill. The first substantive act to be passed, signifying Joey Smallwood's intention to raise a new generation of educated Newfoundlanders, transformed Memorial College into a full-fledged University. Soon after, plans were set afoot to build a new campus and bring in faculty from all over the world. "Memorial will be one of the great small universities of the world," Smallwood said, mixing his favourite oxymorons of great and small. He took a personal hand in the university's financing, and when Montreal fund-raiser, Bill Lawrence, offered to raise a million dollars for Memorial for a fee of thirty thousand dollars, he was promptly invited to come to St. John's. Smallwood sought the biggest name he could get to become chancellor, and after being turned down by Lord Beaverbrook, a Canadian-born British industrialist, and Garfield Weston, another successful Canadian living in England, he finally landed Lord Rothermere, the British newspaper baron. After him, Canadian newspaper magnate Roy Thomson, later Lord Thomson, took on the task of adding prestige and financial clout to Memorial.

Joey Smallwood's second political triumph followed on June 27, a month after the provincial election, when Liberal candidates, again handpicked, won five of the island's seven seats in the federal voting that returned Prime Minister St. Laurent to office. Joey Smallwood was living the dream he'd nurtured since his days at Feild College. He'd become the single unchallenged and dominant political boss of Newfoundland.

The first Dominion Day (later to become known as Canada Day) was marked in Newfoundland on July 1, 1949, three days after the federal election. In other provinces, Canadians celebrated their country's birthday, but in St. John's and across the island, the occasion was overshadowed by sombre Memorial Day services for the gallant men of the Newfoundland Regiment and their incredible heroism in the fighting for the French village of Beaumont-Hamel in the First World War. Of the 801 men who left their trenches to begin the Battle of the Somme on the morning of July 1, 1916, only sixty-nine returned.

Tiring of his two small rooms in the Colonial Building, Joey Smallwood arranged to rent the residential portion of Canada House, a stately mansion on Circular Road that had been the headquarters of the Canadian high commissioner to Newfoundland, a post that no longer existed. Fresh paint only partly revived the faded splendor of its thirty-two rooms. The offices of his Cabinet ministers were scattered around the city, while members of the Assembly scrounged desk space in the Colonial Building. Newsmen mingled with civil servants, and members of the public wandered in and out. While making good use of his quarters at Canada House, Joey for a time turned down other perks, including a government car. But he kept his door open to any visitor and personally took any phone call that came to him. This practice drove his staff crazy; even in the midst of meetings with official visitors, Joey would pick up the phone whenever it rang. He was able to quickly grasp the caller's problem and would call one of his ministers with instructions to take action. Later, Smallwood had an intercom installed at his desk so that he could reach any minister at will — and woe betide the one who wasn't available when he buzzed! When an idea occurred to him during a sleepless night, he'd immediately phone the unfortunate object of his latest scheme. Ministers became accustomed to being awakened at two and three in the morning with orders from Joey to "get right on it."

The first legislature was only a few months old when Joey was taunted in the House one day by an opposition member over his obsession to bring new industries to Newfoundland. "Develop or perish," the taunt went. Joey expropriated the expression and made it the centerpiece of his program. "Newfoundland must develop or perish; we cannot stand still," he told the legislature on July 28, 1949. Newfoundland, like every other underdeveloped country in the middle of the twentieth century, would find its destiny in industrialization. The Soviet Union and China, two Socialist examples, were going down that road, and Smallwood, having set a chain of social reforms in motion, was now ready to use public monies to bring new industries to the province.

In the five years between 1949 and 1954, Smallwood's government injected several hundred million dollars into subsidies for new industries. Newfoundland had two great pulp and paper mills, and Joey wanted a third and a fourth, along with a modernized fishery and hydroelectric development both on the island and in Labrador. His first stimulus program was a three-million-dollar public works program that created nine thousand temporary jobs but hardly dented the 10 percent unemployment rate. A loan fund made loans of fifty thousand dollars to almost anyone with a business plan. Smallwood hoped to attract Canadian and American companies but few were interested in setting up plants so far from major markets.

Into this vacuum drifted Alfred A. Valdmanis, a man of somewhat uncertain European background who had been recommended, according to Smallwood, by C.D. Howe, Ottawa's famous "minister of everything." Smallwood received Valdmanis in his Chateau Laurier hotel room in Ottawa and was beguiled by his story of escape from Latvia during the German occupation in the Second World War. Smallwood thought him "brilliant and knowledgeable" and found space for him in the basement of the Colonial Building, where he set to work in May 1950 as Newfoundland's director of economic development.

Valdmanis had been classically educated and conducted himself with European courtliness. He insisted on addressing Smallwood as "Your Excellency" and "My Premier." This exasperated Joey's ministers but Smallwood loved it. Within months, Valdmanis produced plans for two new industries: a cement mill and a plant producing gypsum wallboard. He scoured Germany, where he had high-level industrial contacts for companies willing to build them — with Newfoundland paying the shot. The government operated them for a while before finding private buyers — in both cases Newfoundland groups — who took them over at a fraction of their cost.

So went the Smallwood "develop or perish" strategy: government money funnelled into projects that either failed or fell into the hands of private companies at much less than their original cost. In the next five years, this strategy led to the establishment of some twenty new industries, of which sixteen were built by German interests. Only a handful survived their initial years. Without such inducements, Smallwood admitted in 1952, "we could not have persuaded one company to come here."

Travelling with Valdmanis on several of his European trips, Joey became acquainted with the postwar leaders of Germany and other countries. He would recall with delight his being introduced at the Frankfurt opera as the minister-president of Newfoundland. It was also during these trips that Smallwood cultivated a serious taste for fine wine; he amazed Sir Leonard Outerbridge, by then a former lieutenant governor, with his detailed knowledge of French winemaking, all of it picked up from books that he'd devoured over the years.

The early years of Smallwood's industrialization campaign failed to dent either the continuing emigration of workers from the province or its unemployment rate. The first year of Confederation was especially difficult; the fishing season was poor; Britain had few dollars to buy Newfoundland fish, newsprint, or iron ore; Bell Island, the site of a large iron ore mine, fell into depression when its British market collapsed; and six hundred workers lost their

Smallwood celebrating the victory of Confederation.

jobs when American military bases closed down. Thousands of workers left to seek jobs in mainland Canada, leading the

Newfoundland Board of Trade to worry about the "almost wholesale migration from Newfoundland" of people it described as "the most ambitious and the most industrious." The media became more critical. "This is the government's most severe test," the *Daily News* wrote on June 2, 1950. "Now the demand is for action and the need was never more urgent."

Partly in response, Joey Smallwood turned his sights from industrialization to mining, announcing "the greatest drive for mineral resources ever experienced in this province." To Joey, living the dream meant taking risks — fifty million dollars of taxpayer money spent on schemes like these would be bound to pay off, one way or another. "Only a few short years ago," he declared, "Newfoundland was not heard of and if known, then as a backward, underdeveloped island. Today she is well known in the circles of industrialists and financiers on both sides of the Atlantic."

Joey Smallwood was ever ready to admit to his failings, but those to which he owned up were largely unfulfilled dreams rather than major policy mistakes. In his memoirs, he regrets his failure to line the Trans-Canada Highway "with flowering trees" and expresses sadness at his inability to find a deserted cove where he could recreate a Newfoundland fishing settlement of the sixteenth century. He failed to get a lot of statues and memorials built in front of the new home of Newfoundland's legislature, the Confederation Building. He missed out on pushing for deep-water oil well drilling. He failed to convince Volkswagen to bring a car assembly plant to Newfoundland, and so his idea of shipping cars up the St. Lawrence River on a government-owned freighter never came to pass. But the dream went on, amid successes and failures, building a new Newfoundland that by the end of Joey Smallwood's life would bear little resemblance to the country he had convinced to join Canada.

7

The Politician's Politician

No deal ever struck between two people brought as much benefit to both as did the agreement Joey Smallwood made to bring his chosen Ottawa emissary, John Whitney Pickersgill, to Newfoundland. When the two first met during Smallwood's 1946 visit to Ottawa, Jack Pickersgill was the cherubic, enthusiastic special assistant to the prime minister of Canada, Mackenzie King. Raised on a farm in Manitoba, "Pick" had graduated from the University of Manitoba and studied at Oxford University. He joined the Department of External Affairs (later to become the Department of Foreign Affairs) but had never run for elective office. Whenever Joey had a problem with Ottawa, he would turn to Pickersgill for help. As Clerk of the Privy Council under Mackenzie King's successor, Louis St. Laurent, no one in Ottawa, short of the prime minister himself, ranked higher or was more influential than Jack Pickersgill.

Both men shared many qualities, including an intense interest in scholarship and history, an aptitude for political intrigue, a focused — if narrow — outlook based on their respective rural and small town upbringings, and a commitment to public service as the highest calling outside the clergy. Their chance meeting in August 1946, when Joey first went to Ottawa to ferret out the workings of the Canadian Confederation, brought them quickly to the realization that they were of similar minds. Later, when the federal Cabinet vacillated over its response to the delegation that the National Convention had sent to Ottawa, Pickersgill was a strong behind-the-scenes advocate for Newfoundland's admission. He and Smallwood were both emotionally committed to nationalism — Smallwood's original fervor for Newfoundland growing gradually into a pan-Canadian nationalism, while Pickersgill from the outset held to the view that allowing Newfoundland to fall under American influence, as had happened in the case of Alaska, would have strangled Canada, "not physically, but spiritually." It was Pickersgill, of course, who convinced Mackenzie King that Newfoundland had voted in sufficient numbers for Confederation to warrant making the deal. If Joey Smallwood can be considered the "last father of Confederation," Jack Pickersgill is surely its latter-day stepfather. "Without him," Smallwood would write in his memoirs, "Newfoundland might not even yet have become a province of Canada."

John Whitney Pickersgill was born on June 23, 1905, at Wycombe, Ontario, the son of a devout Conservative who gave him the name of Sir James Whitney, a Tory premier of Ontario. The family moved west to settle on a three-quarter section homestead near Lake Manitoba. Jack grew up an ardent Tory, but after the death of his father, who had been badly wounded at

Passchendaele while serving with the Canadian Expeditionary Force in the First World War, his interests turned more to the academic life. He was educated at the University of Manitoba and Oxford University, and studied history in Winnipeg. Pickersgill joined the Department of External affairs in Ottawa, and in 1937 he unexpectedly won a competition to become assistant private secretary to Mackenzie King. Colleagues told him he wouldn't last six months, but the job marked the beginning of a remarkable thirty-year career as a mandarin, Member of Parliament, and Cabinet minister.

Joey Smallwood would never forget the support Pickersgill had given him during his first forays to Ottawa. After becoming premier, with Pickersgill now firmly settled in at the head of the Privy Council, Smallwood came to regard the Manitoban as "the best friend [he] had in Ottawa."

When Smallwood had proposed that Gordon Bradley become Newfoundland's representative in the Cabinet with the portfolio of secretary of state, Pickersgill had slapped Joey on the knee and declared, "It's perfect!" Bradley enjoyed the dignity of the post but never really took to life in Ottawa. As he aged, he became less malleable to Smallwood's dictates and pined more for his Newfoundland home. The distance between the two men grew, and Smallwood quit calling on Bradley when he was in Ottawa. One day in 1952, while Joey sat in the visitors' galley of the House of Commons, he was shocked to see that the secretary of state has fallen asleep in his seat. A federal election was looming for 1953, and the incident convinced Smallwood that Newfoundland needed a new man at Ottawa.

In January of that year, Smallwood found himself on another long, slow Trans-Canada Air Lines flight from St. John's to the capital. Even though it was a Saturday, he found Jack

Pickersgill in his Parliament Hill office five doors away from the prime minister. The two went to lunch at the Rideau Club and, after a discussion of possible successors to Bradley, adjourned to Pickersgill's home in the tony suburb of Rockcliffe. They continued to discuss various Newfoundland possibilities, when Smallwood suddenly blurted out, "Jack, if you hadn't taken that Privy Council job, you'd be the ideal man!"

Little had Smallwood realized how his stars were coming into alignment. Pickersgill had in fact become increasingly uneasy at the Privy Council; he was under criticism for turning his position, the highest civil service job in the land, into that of a political functionary. Prime Minister St. Laurent, who Pickersgill feared was showing signs of approaching senility, had been casting about for a constituency in which he could run his favourite mandarin. "Come down to Newfoundland," Joey would have said, or words to that effect, "and take over Bradley's seat — there's no doubt you'll be elected." Smallwood left Pickersgill's house that night with the firm understanding that he had his man. On Monday morning, Pickersgill went to St. Laurent with the scheme. The prime minister enthusiastically approved, and the wheels were set in motion. It took little persuasion for Bradley to accept appointment to the Senate. The three — Smallwood, Pickersgill, and Bradley — flew to London in May to represent their province at the coronation of Queen Elizabeth. At a meeting in Pickersgill's hotel room, they drafted Bradley's letter of resignation and Pickersgill's acceptance of the nomination. Smallwood would have Pick run in Bradley's old seat of Bonavista–Twillingate. On October 10, 1953, Pickersgill received more than ten thousand votes, four times the number of his opponent. Joey Smallwood's candidates had swept all seven Newfoundland seats in the general election. Pickersgill would win the seat by comfortable margins in five more elections.

Joey Smallwood says not a word in his memoirs about how he recruited Jack Pickersgill to a partnership that became one of the most successful in Canadian history. He did, however, concede that Pickersgill was "the most brilliant man" he knew in Canadian politics." Pickersgill, for his part, became the complete Newfoundlander. He bought a house in his riding and spent the summers travelling the coast, often aboard his 125-ton schooner, the *Millie Ford*. He enrolled his son at Memorial University, and his daughter took up the practice of medicine in Gander.

In a federation where powers were split between Ottawa and the provinces and the federal authority still held up the upper hand, few major projects could go forward without at least the tacit agreement of the federal government. Pickersgill took over Bradley's old post as secretary of state in June, 1953, four months in advance of that year's general election. Smallwood used the time to sing Pickersgill's praises in Newfoundland, and when the campaign came, he was at Pickersgill's side, introducing him to voters throughout Bonavista–Twillingate. The campaign was as colorful as it was crucial to Smallwood's plans for his new partner's political future. As they went from outport to outport, raucous welcomes greeted the comrades in arms. Smallwood had a Salvation Army band on the dock at Twillingate, playing "Hold the Fort for I am Coming." Salvos from a 240-year-old cannon announced their arrival in Fogo.

Even before the election, the benefits of Pickersgill's connection with Newfoundland were flowing to the island. Spending on such federal installations as docks and post offices went up immediately. Later, Ottawa paid 90 percent of the cost to complete the island's section of the Trans-Canada Highway, with Picksergill bestowing other favours, such as subsidies to bail out a failing Newfoundland airline. A longer-term benefit came in the extension of unemployment insurance to fishermen, which was soon running into millions of dollars a year.

For all their similarities, Smallwood and Pickersgill could display distinctly different personalities. Smallwood was the more volatile and mercurial of the two, while Pickersgill acted as a moderating influence, perhaps the result of the training he'd received at the hands of Mackenzie King, the compromiser *par excellence* of Canadian politics. Both could be emotional. Joey would stand voiceless at the playing of "O Canada" or "Ode to Newfoundland"; he knew that if he started singing, he'd be overcome with sentiment. Pickersgill was equally sentimental on matters that affected him deeply. "You will never know how much I owe you," he would tell Newfoundland voters, tears in his eyes.

Perhaps one reason for Jack Pickersgill's sentimentality lay in a shadow that hovered over his life. In it was enshrined the tragic memory of his younger brother, Frank, a footloose freelance journalist who had tramped around Europe in the 1930s. He was caught in France by the German invasion, escaped to England, and then joined the Canadian Intelligence Corps with the rank of captain. With a fellow Canadian, John Macalister, he parachuted into the Loire Valley in 1943 to work with the French Resistance. It was an assignment for which both were ill-prepared. They were soon betrayed and captured at a German checkpoint. Frank Pickersgill tried to escape the prison in Paris where they were held, but was shot and recaptured. Later, both were sent to the infamous Nazi concentration camp at Buchenwald. The pair died there on September 14, 1944, hung on meat hooks and strangled with piano wire. Jack Pickersgill rarely spoke of his brother's fate. Even after a collection of Frank's letters was published in 1948, few Canadians were aware of the tragic circumstances of his death.

What ultimately united Pickersgill and Smallwood in a new common cause was the defeat of the federal Liberals in 1957 and the election of a Progressive Conservative government, with John Diefenbaker as prime minister. During that campaign, Pickersgill had declared: "It is not merely for the well-being of Canadians but for the good of mankind in general that the present Liberal government should remain in office." The Liberals were, after all, the natural governing party. The defeat brought out a streak of violent partisanship in Pickersgill; he resented losing control of the levers of power, saw the Conservatives as a party of Anglo-Saxon racists, and thought that nothing Diefenbaker might do was right. With a voice described as something between a cackle and a quack, Pickersgill was on his feet day after day in Parliament, tormenting Diefenbaker and his ministers. His normally cherubic face would screw up with a scowl as he peered at the government benches through his rimless glasses. The frequency of his sallies would earn him the nickname "Jumping Jack."

In all the years that Pickersgill and Smallwood piloted the political destiny of Newfoundland — during their informal relationship between their meeting in 1946 and Pickersgill's arrival as a Newfoundland MP in 1953, and from that date until Pickersgill's retirement in 1967 — the two often had minor disagreements. Pickersgill was never comfortable with some of the questionable characters that Joey Smallwood tolerated in his drive to develop new industries. Whatever portfolio Pickersgill held made little difference in their partnership. His position as minister of citizenship and immigration between 1954 and 1957 put him in a portfolio of no great significance to Newfoundland. Islanders were not anxious to encourage immigration, nor did many new arrivals care to settle there. It was Pickersgill's influence as the "political minister" of Newfoundland that counted.

Almost from the beginning of Diefenbaker's tenure, the new Conservative government had run into problems in Newfoundland. There were arguments over Term 29, with Pickersgill and Smallwood leading the attack against Diefenbaker's decision to stop Ottawa's annual eight-million-dollar payment to Newfoundland as of 1962. After bitter controversy, they got a five-year extension. When a strike of International Woods Workers of America (IWA) shook Newfoundland in 1959, many in the Liberal opposition were critical of Joey Smallwood's aggressive assault on the union. Jack Pickersgill stood with Smallwood, threatening to take Newfoundland Liberal MPs out of the party if the Liberals did not support their Newfoundland ally. But it was in the flag debate, when Smallwood — as a traditional British monarchist — opposed the replacement of the Union Jack with a Maple Leaf flag, that Pickersgill proved his real worth. He had supported the new flag just as strongly as Smallwood had opposed it. But Pickersgill mediated a compromise that saw Smallwood accept the new flag, while Newfoundland retained the Union Jack as its own provincial flag. Without the support of Newfoundland MPs (all under the influence of Smallwood) on the flag vote, the Liberal minority government of Lester Pearson would almost certainly have fallen.

It was manoeuvers such as these that transformed Jack Pickersgill into the politicians' politician — a man who could deal with his peers as effectively as with his constituents, and gain the results he wanted. His standing in Ottawa, even during the years the Liberals were in opposition to Prime Minister Diefenbaker, set him apart from most MPs. His encyclopedic knowledge of Parliamentary procedure, his mastery of bureaucratic methods learned as a civil servant, his effective front-bench criticism of his Conservative opponents, and his staunch support of Newfoundland interests all combined to make him a hero to Smallwood. "This is Pickersgill!" Smallwood would exclaim in introducing him at public rallies. "Isn't that an incredible name! You'd better like him despite his name. He's the second-most important man in Canada ... someday he'll be Prime Minister!"

That would never come to pass, and along the way Pickersgill would commit his share of blunders. His advice to St. Laurent to impose closure in the great Pipeline Debate of 1956 played a big part in the Liberals' disaster at the polls the next year. In an equally inept move, Pickersgill authored Lester Pearson's 1957 non-confidence motion, moved early in the life of the first Diefenbaker minority government, calling on the Conservatives to resign and turn power back to the Liberals. It gave John Diefenbaker a golden opportunity to campaign against Liberal arrogance and is credited with helping the Conservatives to win the 1958 election by the greatest majority in Canadian history.

Jack Pickersgill found himself back in the Cabinet with the election of Lester Pearson as prime minister in 1963, first as secretary of state and House leader, and then as minister of transport. By the mid-1960s, Pickersgill recognized the clock was running down on the Joey Smallwood era, just as he had sensed the days were numbered for the St. Laurent government a decade earlier. Over a three-year period from 1964 to 1967, he piloted new legislation governing transport regulation in

Canada, covering everything from ship traffic to airline fares and railway operations. The bill created a new agency, the Canadian Transport Commission, and Pickersgill had himself appointed to its forty-thousand-dollar-a-year chairmanship. For a man known for his frugality — he had once submitted an expense account of $30.35 for a twelve-day trip to British Columbia — it marked a breathtaking leap to financial security.

Joey Smallwood presided over an elaborate retirement dinner for Pickersgill in September 1967, and the Newfoundland government established in his name a four-thousand-dollar scholarship for a Memorial University graduate to study history or political science. Between 1960 and 1970, Pickersgill, with historian D. F. Forster, produced *The Mackenzie King Record,* a four-volume series that drew substantially from the late prime minister's diary. They carefully excised all mention of King's pursuit of spiritualism, visits by mediums to his home, or his attempts to communicate with his long-dead mother or various dogs, all called Pat. It was not until 1976 that Canadians became generally aware, through military historian C.P. Stacey's book, *A Very Double Life: The Private World of Mackenzie King,* of their late prime minister's passion for the occult. The disclosures earned King the nickname "Weird Willie."

How many other secrets did Pickersgill hold on to? How involved was he in the calamitous negotiations with Quebec over the ill-fated Churchill Falls hydro project? To what extent did his decision to get out of politics contribute to the decline and eventual demise of Joey Smallwood's political dynasty? That was a story yet to be told.

8

Fouling the Nest

If Joey Smallwood's partnership with Jack Pickersgill was the most successful of his political life, his relationship with Alfred Valdmanis was surely the most disastrous. What is worse, Smallwood's recruitment of the former Latvian *wunderkind* (boy wonder) led, directly and indirectly, to the entrenchment of a circle of larcenous, plundering, and predatory adventurers eager to take advantage of the Newfoundland government's obsession to bring new industries to the island.

From the first meeting of the two men in the premier's Ottawa hotel room in 1950, Smallwood seems to have fallen under the spell of the inscrutable Valdmanis's tales: his upbringing, his suffering during successive Soviet and German occupations, and his struggle to rebuild his life after the war. He had enjoyed a promising boyhood in his native country, he told Smallwood, having earned degrees in economics and philosophy as well as a doctorate in law from the University of Frankfurt. At the age of twenty-nine, he was appointed minister of finance and trade of Latvia. Then came the war and first Soviet occupation, followed by the German invasion that marked Hitler's attack on the Soviet Union. As Valdmanis told the story, he was arrested and tortured by the Russians, then jailed by the Germans as a leader of Latvian resistance. Others would picture the young Valdmanis as a willing collaborator with both; after having worked with the Russians, he became a director of justice under the Germans, extracting himself from two years of collaboration through the help of a German banker who arranged his transfer to the Reich. There were allegations, later retracted, that he had participated in the killing of Jews. Valdmanis spent the last years of the war in Germany. In the chaos of postwar Europe, his immigration to Canada was facilitated by contacts he established among Canadians in the International Refugee Organization.

Valdmanis was not a physically impressive man, but he bore a serious face and a fierce gaze that conveyed a sense of intense concentration and total self-confidence, all characteristics of the charismatic manipulator. Smallwood is reputed to have said of him, "I loved him as I loved no brother or sister of my own."

Working out of a small basement office in the Colonial Building, Valdmanis would have led a lonely life in St. John's. His previous Canadian jobs as a visiting professor at Carleton College in Ottawa and McGill University in Montreal had at least put him in academic environments. In St. John's Valdmanis would live in rented rooms, his European background leaving him ill-fitted to socialize with Newfoundlanders — other than a few government officials — conditioned by a vastly different cultural experience. Adding to Valdmanis's loneliness would have been the fact that his wife Irma stayed in Montreal — no woman accustomed to the social milieu of the salons of Europe was going to be content in such a primitive outpost.

Working in twelve hour stretches, at the beck of Joey Smallwood nights as well as days, Valdmanis devised a financing formula that would enable the government to stretch the six million dollars that had been earmarked to aid new industries. Valdmanis recommended the government put up only half the money for new projects, with private investors being credited the other half through machinery and technical know-how they would provide. The strategy was going to open the door to vast new industries: steel, chemicals, pulp, and paper. It was an accounting formula tailor-made for abuse, but for a time, it worked. Smallwood soon increased his economic director's salary to twenty-five thousand dollars a year.

Joey Smallwood accompanied Valdmanis on several of his investor hunting trips to Europe, which involved elaborate state dinners, long meetings, visits to the opera, and receptions at the ornate homes of millionaire industrialists. While Smallwood was treated respectfully during all these visits, he must have had second thoughts about the details of the deals that were being discussed. Most negotiations took place in German and Smallwood had to rely on Valdmanis to translate what had been said.

It was during one of their European trips that Joey Smallwood decided it was time to call an election, the first since Confederation in 1949. He wanted a mandate, he told his companions at a breakfast in the Grand Hotel in Stockholm, to pursue his "develop or perish" policy. It may not have been a coincidence that the government was running out of cash. Back in St. John's, Smallwood opened a session of the legislature with a throne speech that boasted "Newfoundland has never known such a high degree of prosperity." A week later, he dissolved the House of Assembly and called an election for November 26, 1951. The Conservatives tried to make much of a scandal involving a Dr. Luther Sennewald of Germany. He was ready, the Conservatives alleged, to reveal "surprising manipulations" in the financing of new industries. Dr. Sennewald's threat led not to any public disclosure, but to the granting of a loan of one hundred thousand dollars to set up a plant to make eye glass lenses. There was no scandal, but when it was discovered after the election that Sennewald was removing the funds from an approved bank account, Smallwood sent his executive assistant, Gordon Pushie, to demand an explanation. There was none. Threatened with arrest, Sennewald returned to St. John's with the funds in a suitcase. It was, according to Smallwood biographer Richard Gwyn, the "the only one hundred per cent loan refund on the new industries program." None of it made much difference in the election; Smallwood's Liberals picked up one seat and the Conservatives lost one. It was now full speed ahead in the pursuit of new industry.

Euphoric at the election outcome, Smallwood and Valdmanis concocted a new scheme together for the promotion of industry. It was an early version of the public-private partnership (PPP) that would prove so appealing to some Canadian governments fifty years later. Their version was the Newfoundland and Labrador Corporation (NALCO), 90 percent owned by the Newfoundland government and 10 percent by private investors. Valdmanis had already spelled out what would become the strategy in a December, 1950, memo to his premier: "What we need is American interest, American names — the bigger politically or economically the better and their even if only token participation, because once we have their names, then for the sake of their own names they cannot let us down."

The bill establishing NALCO passed the House of Assembly only after tumultuous debate. The opposition called it "pure gamble and speculation." Smallwood recruited Sir William Stephenson, Canada's famed Second World War spymaster (the model for "M" of the James Bond novels) as chairman. Stephenson decided to raise ten million dollars by selling bonds, using the money to buy the three government-owned plants that had so far been built. Not a single buyer took the bait, and seven months later Smallwood was looking for a new chairman.

A new instrument was needed if Newfoundland was to attract the millions of dollars needed for its new era of industrial prosperity. On December 24, 1952, Smallwood announced the creation of the British Newfoundland Development Corporation (BRINCO). It would be modelled along the lines of the ancient East India Company and the Hudson's Bay Company — a consortium of wealthy investors representing "the biggest combination of industrial and financial interests ever brought together in the world's history for prospecting and developing natural resources."

It had long been a dream of Joey Smallwood to organize such a vast array of wealth for the purpose of remaking modern Newfoundland. He'd talked over the idea with Sir Winston Churchill, who saw it as "a great Imperial enterprise." With Churchill's encouragement, he'd gained the support of N.M. Rothchild and Sons, the English banking firm. Once BRINCO was established, most of the prime holdings that had been assigned to NALCO, including Churchill Falls — a potential hydro power site in Labrador — were transferred to it.

It was around this time that Joey Smallwood began to wonder what he was getting for all the millions he had been investing in the new companies formed under Valdmanis's watch. Their work of four years had led to the creation of around twenty companies at the cost to the government of some fifty million dollars. Most were by now floundering. Where Smallwood had once been charmed by Valdmanis's social skills in tennis, dancing, and singing, and his ability to speak half a dozen languages, he now grew irritated at his protege's autocratic and often unpredictable behaviour.

Smallwood decided to wind up NALCO in April 1953. Having lost faith in Valdmanis, he expressed no objection when, in June 1953, the Latvian resigned as economic director. As a consolation, Smallwood agreed to allow him to preside over a campaign to sell NALCO shares. Canadian Javelin Foundries, a little-known company run by one John Christopher Doyle, signed up to buy most of its stock. The deal collapsed when Canadian Javelin's shares were delisted after having taken investors for rollercoaster rides on the Toronto and Montreal Stock Exchanges. Still looking for a buyer, Valdmanis moved NALCO's head office to Montreal. In February 1954 he flew back to St. John's for a round of meetings, including one with Joey Smallwood. Striding into the premier's office, he held out his hand in greeting. Smallwood kept his hands by his side. "I want your resignation," he told Valdmanis, "and I want it right away." Stunned, Valdmanis could only answer, "Yes, my premier."

Valdmanis never asked why he was being dismissed, probably because he suspected the cause: he'd been padding his expense accounts. He'd been found out by one of Joey Smallwood's most trusted confidantes, Greg Power. Valdmanis had been collecting two salaries, one as head of NALCO and the other as director of economic development. It was also found out that he had passed off personal expenses, including the cost of a new car, charges for hotel suites, and furniture bought for his Montreal home, to his office budgets. While these abuses combined with Smallwood's dissatisfaction with his performance were sufficient to warrant dismissal, worse was yet to come: secret midnight drives around St. John's, Smallwood at the wheel, a whistle-blower filling him with alarming details of Valdmanis's corruption. The informer, a Latvian engineer who had had a falling-out with his countryman, revealed Valdmanis had been skimming commissions off government grants to German companies. He'd been telling them the money was for donations to the Liberal Party. Knowing the party had never received them, Smallwood called the Royal Canadian Mounted Police.

By the time the RCMP had completed their investigation, Joey Smallwood was ready to go public. Valdmanis had been picked up at the St. Andrews, New Brunswick, home of his brother Osvald, who managed a fishery plant there. Smallwood tipped a Canadian Press reporter to Valdmanis's arrest and issued a statement saying he'd been taken into custody for having "extorted very large sums of money from various firms with whom he dealt in behalf of the Government of Newfoundland." The news set off a national uproar. The opposition demanded, unsuccessfully, a Royal Commission inquiry. At Valdmanis's trial, he was charged with fraudulently obtaining $470,000 from two German companies involved in building the gypsum and cement plants that had inaugurated Smallwood's drive for new industry. The money, of course, came from the government grants Valdmanis had obtained for them. Chief Justice Sir Albert Walsh sentenced him to four years in Her Majesty's Penitentiary. The court seized Valdmanis's investments, valued at more than $500,000, but only $13,000 was ever recovered. What happened to the rest of the money would never be determined. Payments had been deposited to an American Express account in New York in the name of the sister of Valdmanis's wife. The FBI secretly photographed the records, and there was talk of blackmail. Valdmanis gave interviews in jail, speaking of Smallwood as a friend that he was certain would support him. He returned to Montreal after his release on parole in 1956 and set up an export-import business. Little more was heard of Valdmanis until he was killed in a car accident near Edmonton, Alberta, on August 11, 1970.

To Joey Smallwood, the entire episode had been "a shattering experience." On hearing of his death, he commented that Valdmanis was "a brilliant but tragic figure."

The ill-gotten gains of Alfred Valdmanis were nothing, however, compared to the three hundred million dollars in public funds squandered by John Doyle, a fast-talking, high-living promoter born in Chicago to Canadian parents. Before coming to Newfoundland, he'd sold coal in Western Canada and had run a stove-making business in Joliette, Quebec, that became Canadian Javelin Limited. After Doyle's deed to buy NALCO shares fell through, the Newfoundland government was looking for a way to dispose of mineral rights to a 2,400-square-mile tract of land near Lake Wabush, in central Labrador, that had been turned back by the Iron Ore Company of Canada. It was busy developing a fabulous ore find at Knob Lake and had no time for the doubtful Lake Wabush property. Doyle put two and two together, and in 1953, when Joey Smallwood offered him the concession, he grabbed it. A fifteen million dollar survey turned up evidence of a two billion ton ore bonanza. With Smallwood's help, Doyle put together a new company, Wabush Iron, which he sold off over a period of six years to an international consortium that invested 235 million dollars to complete a plant and mill. Doyle's payout amounted to tens of millions of dollars.

While the deal made Doyle wealthy, it failed to gain Newfoundland the high-end processing plant Smallwood had wanted. Under pressure from Quebec, Wabash Iron had agreed to locate its pelletizing plant, where iron ore would be readied for refining, at Pointe Noire. Smallwood wanted it built in Newfoundland, telling the legislature, "I am prepared to stand or fall on this." He recruited Jack Pickersgill to the cause, calling once again on his Ottawa ally to rescue him. Try as he would, there was nothing Pickersgill could do. Wabush Iron threatened to move the entire project to the United States if it couldn't put the pellet plant in Quebec. As a consolation, the company returned to Newfoundland NALCO, the much-travelled company it had inherited in its deal with Doyle.

The Wabush Iron mine officially opened on July 20, 1964. "Never in the history of Newfoundland's industry was so much owed to the effort of one man," Smallwood declared. John Doyle was not present for the celebration. He was in a Hartford, Connecticut, court, charged on eleven counts of violating U.S. security regulations. Joey Smallwood had done everything he could to rescue his friend, including making a fruitless visit to Washington, D.C., to see Robert Kennedy, then attorney general of the United States. Smallwood noted in his diary that Kennedy was "very pleasant. Very keen and … a very bright fellow." But Kennedy declined to interfere in the case. When Doyle went to trial, he pleaded guilty and was sentenced to three months in prison. Rather than serve the time, he jumped bail and returned to Canada. Forever after, he would be fugitive from U.S. justice.

It was not the first time he had been in such trouble. He'd earlier been arraigned in Montreal on charges of theft and fraud involving nearly five million dollars worth of mining stock. He'd launched and defended numerous lawsuits and fought back against Revenue Canada's claims that he'd fallen millions of dollars short in tax payments.

Up to this point, the various schemes Doyle had wangled through Smallwood had earned Newfoundland a modest number of new mining jobs but not much in the way of royalties and taxes. The two continued to fly about the world (carefully avoiding the United States) in Doyle's DC-6 aircraft, tarted up with mahogany fittings and a crystal chandelier. Minor scandals involving Doyle and the federal and Quebec Liberal parties came and went. Joey Smallwood continued to dream of building a third great pulp and paper plant in Newfoundland. The first two, at Grand Falls and Cornerbrook, had been established by Joey's heroes, Sir Richard Bond and Sir Richard Squires. Matching their achievements would mark a fitting climax to the Smallwood saga.

In 1967 the House of Assembly approved an investment of fifty-three million dollars toward the building of a linerboard mill to make corrugated paper in Stephenville, in western Newfoundland. The government's partner would be one of John Doyle's companies, Melville Pulp and Paper. Because Melville Pulp had cutting rights in the Goose Bay area of Labrador, it was decided to ship wood chips from there to Stephenville, a distance of a thousand kilometres across land and water. From the beginning, the scheme was a fiasco. Thousands of cords of wood were washed overboard when barges hit heavy weather. By 1972, Newfoundland's investment had reached $122 million, but Smallwood was out of office. The Conservative government of Frank Moores bought the plant and by the time it was finally sold to Abitibi-Consolidated, the cost to Newfoundland had reached the $300 million mark. The plant operated as a pulp mill until it was demolished in 2008, only an empty field remaining where a bustling processing mill, smokestacks, and storage bins had once stood.

The Stephenville affair had left such a stench that in 1973 the RCMP raided Doyle's apartment in Montreal. They found evidence to indict him on four hundred counts of fraud and breach of trust relating to the linerboard plant. Other embarrassing documents were turned up. A list was found of payments that were supposedly to be made by Doyle, including $375,000 to a Mr. J.R. Smallwood and $175,000 to a Mr. L.R. Curtis (Leslie Curtis had been attorney general of Newfoundland). Doyle was taken to St. John's, where after a weekend in jail he was released on $75,000 bail. He never came to trial. Doyle fled Canada and spent the rest of his life in Panama. While there, the Quebec Superior Court found Doyle had defrauded Javelin investors and ordered him to pay $15.4 million in damages. From Panama, Doyle backed mining explorations throughout South America and continued his flamboyant lifestyle, making headlines along the way. He would die in Panama in 2000, never having answered to his various crimes and misdemeanors, leaving in his wake a trail of exploited investors victimized by boiler-shop stock frauds, insider trading abuses, unpaid government loans, and corporate intrigue.

Joey Smallwood's tolerance for high-living characters like John Doyle and Alfred Valdmanis who came to Newfoundland offering much but delivering little raises questions about his judgment and his ability to distinguish between the bogus and the genuine, between bravado and reality. Was he naive when it came to measuring men, or was he driven by his delight in having around him people of material wealth and intellectual accomplishment? Clyde Wells, who joined the Smallwood Cabinet many years later and served as premier from 1989 to 1996, sees the Valdmanis affair as something that could have happened to anyone. "All of us run into a crook, and can get taken in. That doesn't mean you stop dealing with people. You get on with your life. While you probably should be more alert, you don't stop doing things."

Others have expressed a different take on Smallwood's relationship with Doyle. Harold Horwood wrote that "none of his (Smallwood's) many close partnerships was happier or more productive." John Crosbie, who as a Smallwood Cabinet minister tried to negotiate with Doyle, has described the relationship between the two as "one of the most tawdry stories in twentieth-century provincial politics." Joey Smallwood was never implicated in any of John Doyle's questionable financial dealings and no evidence was ever presented that he had received any payment from him. The opposition howled throughout these controversies, but their protests had no effect on the outcome of the five provincial elections won by Joey Smallwood between 1951 and 1966. The nest may have been fouled, but the eggs continued to hatch.

9

Of Family and Fortune

On Sunday, May 12, 1957, Joey Smallwood gathered his family about him at Russwood Ranch, a farm set in the rolling hills bordering Roache's Line, a dirt-and-gravel trail that ran south of Brigus, a fishing village on Conception Bay. Joey and his wife Clara had driven the eighty kilometres from their official residence, Canada House in St. John's, looking forward to a pleasant weekend. Waiting for them were their daughter Clara and her husband Ed Russell, as well as eldest son Ramsay, his wife Florence, and Florence's twin sister Dorcas Marro, who was visiting from New Hampshire. Ed and Clara had lived at Russwood Ranch since its beginning and pretty well ran the spread. After taking a quick look at the site for a new house that Joey intended to call Newfoundland House, they talked about the festive Mother's Day dinner to take place later that day on the ranch.

Joey Smallwood had planned a special highlight: a demonstration by Eastern Provincial Airways of one of its helicopters, a Bell A7J Ranger, that would be going into service as an air ambulance for the provincial government. The machine landed near the entrance to the ranch at about eleven o'clock. The minister of health, Dr. James McGrath, was due along about noon, and while they waited, EPA official Bill Harris explained how the craft would ferry patients on life-saving emergency flights. That done, he invited the premier and his family to go aloft. It would be their first chance to see from the air the nearly six hundred hectares of meadows, creeks, and ponds that Ed Russell and Clara had been working on since 1951, clearing the land and setting up barns for sheep, pigs, and poultry.

Joey Smallwood was no stranger to helicopter flights, and Mrs. Smallwood was hardly entranced by the idea of a helicopter ride. They thought it a good idea for Ramsay and Florence to go up instead, and suggested Florence's sister go with them. They all climbed aboard and the pilot, Gilbert Wass, revved the engine for takeoff. As he did so, Bill Harris, standing nearby, drew Wass's attention to overhead power lines that ran close to the helicopter. Wass nodded in response, the helicopter's blades spun faster, and the craft quickly became airborne. Within seconds it collided with the six-thousand volt high-tension wires. The impact sheared off the main rotor blade and the machine flipped over, burst into flames, and fell to the ground.

Ed Russell and Reg Smallwood, Joey's brother who worked at the ranch, were the first to reach the helicopter. They pulled Dorcas Marro, and then Ramsay, from their seats. Nothing could be done for Ramsay's wife and the pilot, who had both died almost instantly. Ramsay was horribly burned. Joey managed to get his son into his car and set off for the General

Hospital in St. John's. He was later flown to the burn unit of a hospital in Toronto. Joey, setting aside his government responsibilities, would spend two weeks at his son's bedside. Ramsay survived and returned to Russwood, where he would live quietly and eventually remarry. Pilot Wass, who had flown Lancaster bombers during the war, had joined EPA only three weeks before. His most recent assignment had been to fly Jack Pickersgill around his Newfoundland riding.

For a man who had devoted little time to his wife and children during his years of scrabbling out a living as a union organizer and a journalist, and later as a politician ever-attentive to his voters, Joey Smallwood took an inordinate pride in his family and his home. He recognized that his life would have come asunder without the support of Clara, who in her quiet and dignified way saw to the tranquility of their home and the children's education and upbringing.

The tragedy of Mother's Day 1957 occurred as his daughter Clara and Ed Russell finally had Russwood Ranch running profitably. On a bluff called The Lookout, Ed had put up a life-sized wooden horse that became known as Joey's Horse. Weather-beaten and often attacked by vandals, it crumbled to the ground after ten years. Smallwood always addressed the farm hands as "Mr.," but they found his presence intimidating. They belonged to what he called "the ragged assed artillery," his affectionate term for working-class Newfoundlanders. When he saw a greenhouse attendant asleep on the job, he said nothing but tapped on the glass. The startled attendant later confessed, "He's such a little man but he scares me so much!"

Newfoundland House was laid out in the shape of an arrowhead, with two wings built of glass and chrome, each having its own stairway that descended to a common landing. It all had a Frank Lloyd Wright look about it. In 1959, when they moved in, Joey installed a pair of entry pillars he'd acquired from the old post office on Water Street. Two iron pedestrian gates bore the initials NH inside a circle. After they took up full-time residence, Joey would drive himself into St. John's in the morning, and unless he had to stay in the capital, he usually returned around six o'clock. Security was practically non-existent: "We didn't bother to lock our doors in those days," granddaughter Dale Russell FitzPatrick, daughter of Clara Russell, recalls. The RCMP tried to keep an eye on him in case they were ever needed. After an escaped mental patient went looking for him, the police gave Joey a handgun. His son Bill tried to coach him to load and fire it, but he wasn't interested. He tossed the gun into the backseat of his car and never touched it. (Joey also abandoned piano lessons after a few weeks of fretful practice.) During the FLQ crisis in October 1970, he was given bodyguards.

Joey filled his basement library with as many as eighteen thousand books, hundreds of which arrived in crates from second-hand bookstores he'd visited on his foreign trips. Clara, a voracious reader herself, especially of English history, organized the books and often fell asleep in her favourite chair, one in her lap. Joey would select a dozen or so at a time and pile them beside his bed, usually getting through a stack in less than a week. He had a La-Z-Boy chair set up in a corner of the living room facing a picture window, with a drafting table that swung across his lap. Here he would spend evenings reviewing reports and making notes while receiving and making phone calls. It was often after midnight before he got to bed, and then he'd read for an hour or two before falling sleep.

Whether Joey planned it or not, the two wings of Newfoundland House became virtually separate homes for himself and

Clara as their lives diverged, although they continued to live together contentedly. Her interest in politics dwindled, perhaps due to her chronic bronchitis that often caused coughing spasms during his speeches. More and more, daughter Clara stood in at public events. Mrs. Smallwood cared for orchids, tomatoes, and cacti in her greenhouse and enjoyed playing the piano, but remained as willful as ever, referring to Joey as "Mr. Smallwood" when she was upset with him. After the Smallwoods acquired a Florida condo, she would refuse to go there unless it was for at least two weeks. "It's not worth packing my bags for anything less," she would say. She preferred to go to London, where she would visit art galleries and museums.

Dale Russell FitzPatrick and Ramsay's son Joe (Joseph Smallwood II) recall their days at Newfoundland House as among the happiest of their lives. "We loved to visit Poppy and Mamie," said Dale, referring to the family names for her grandparents. Dale and her cousins frolicked largely unsupervised, horseback riding, canoeing and boating, and driving cars at an early age. Her earliest memories are of Saturday night movies when everyone would gather in the library. Dale and other grandchildren arrived in their pajamas. They loved films featuring Ma and Pa Kettle and Danny Kaye, and Joe says their grandfather never disappointed them. He had the house wired throughout with speakers in an early version of "surround sound." "It sometimes felt as if you were in Carnegie Hall," Joe remembers. Joey often took the children and grandchildren on flights in his friend John Shaheen's Lear Jet to Ottawa, Montreal, and New York. Especially exciting was the time Joey had everyone flown to Expo '67 in Montreal. "We weren't a spoiled middle class family," Dale insists. "We were a down-to-earth family at a time when parents did not feel they had to guard their children day and night."

The Expo visit produced a bonus for Newfoundland when Joey wondered what would become of the temporary pavilions constructed for the event. Told they would be dismantled, he arranged to have two of them taken apart piece by piece and shipped to Newfoundland. Winterized and rebuilt, the Czech pavilion was transformed into the Gordon Pinsent Centre for the Arts in Gander, and the Yugoslav building became the J.R. Smallwood Arts and Cultural Centre in Grand Falls.

As with many families, embarrassments as well as tragedies beset the Smallwoods. In 1967 Joey's son William, a lawyer and a Liberal member of the House of Assembly, became involved in a bitter custody battle with his estranged wife, Marva. The *Evening Telegram* published details of the case, something no Newfoundland newspaper had ever done before. The scandal cost William his bid for re-nomination as a Liberal MHA. Tragedy would strike the family in 1973 when the body of Ed Russell, daughter Clara's husband, would be found in a field on Russwood Ranch. His death was ruled the result of a self-inflicted gunshot wound.

As the grandchildren grew up and Joey Smallwood's time in office lengthened to ten, fifteen, and more years, the effects of his political fortunes would be felt more strongly at Newfoundland House. Controversy over his policies — from spending millions on new industry to moving the residents of isolated outports to larger towns — brought vilification as well as praise. One of Joey's grandchildren dropped out of Memorial University after being harassed by fellow students and professors. "He educated the young and they turned against him," Dale Russell FitzPatrick remembers. Not carrying the Smallwood name, she found, was a social advantage. She once volunteered as a reader at "A Night of Letters to Joey," an evening devoted to the reading of letters women had written to Smallwood. "Those letters gave me an insight into all manner of problems people would write to him about." Only after the reading, while speaking with a woman whose father had worked with and admired Joey, did she admit she was his granddaughter.

Throughout his life, Joey Smallwood paid little attention to his financial fortunes. His wife could recall at least one Christmas in the 1930s when she had to tell the children, "Santa didn't come." His income probably peaked during his Barrelman broadcasts, and as premier he never took home much more than ten thousand dollars a year. In retirement, he boasted that he enjoyed "a handsome and adequate income" of twenty-eight thousand dollars a year from pensions and an investment in a chain of gas stations. Never included in his income, however, were the many perks and favours he received in office — many legitimate but some questionable — including junkets before and after retirement to such places as Russia, China, and Cuba. Corporate friends ferried him about on their jets, a common practice for public figures of that era. The cost of building Newfoundland House was met in part by a thirteen-thousand-dollar mortgage but was eased considerably by gifts from companies doing business with the provincial government. According to John Crosbie, the swimming pool was paid for by one of the Crosbie family companies.

Simple things brought him the most happiness, Smallwood claimed. His greatest "gladness," he would write, came from his children and grandchildren, his first honorary degree, receiving his 33rd degree, Masonic, and being able to bring in mothers' allowances and student aid. His most emotional moments included signing the terms of Confederation, meeting Winston Churchill and Chiu En-lai, and watching Pierre Trudeau win the leadership of the Liberal Party. His greatest elation came from listening to Liszt's Hungarian Rhapsody no. 2 in Budapest, being on the platform with Billy Graham in Ottawa, and attending the coronation of Queen Elizabeth II.

Joey Smallwood never admitted to being challenged by alcohol, but he never forgot how drink had ruined his father's life. It took many years for Joey to overcome his early aversion, although when he did, he became a connoisseur of all types of spirits other than hard liquor. His encyclopedic knowledge of wine and liqueurs is well known, but no one among the hundreds of people with whom he had close connections has ever claimed to have seen him overindulge. He took a personal interest in the stocking of Newfoundland government liquor stores and turned to John Doyle, the controversial mining promoter, for advice on what brands should be listed. The stores soon became known for having one of the best selections of wine in Canada.

During his years as premier, the face of Joey Smallwood became familiar to Canadians through the thousands of pictures of him that appeared on their television screens and in magazines and newspapers. His sharply etched features made him photogenic, and he was never known to turn away from a camera. There was only one widely published photo he didn't like. It showed a sinister-looking Joey Smallwood wearing a florid bow tie and horn-rimmed glasses, a smile bordering on a smirk, his hair combed straight back, while he smoked from an ornate cigarette holder. He could have been a master magician in a circus poster or an Italian count ready to play the gaming tables of Monte Carlo. Ed Roberts, his onetime executive assistant and a successor as Liberal Party leader, likes to point with a smile to a photo in his study of Joey giving a speech in the House of Assembly. In the picture are half a dozen Cabinet ministers, their heads sagging, some staring vacantly off into space, paying no attention whatsoever to him — they'd heard it all before.

As his political fortunes rose and fell, Joey Smallwood remained resigned to his often expressed view that "too many people are eager to believe that every politician is a crook, at heart a thief and embezzler, a rogue and a skunk." He preferred to ignore his critics. "Defending yourself only attracts more attacks and more attention," he would say. "My misfortune as a politician was that there was no other Premier with whom Newfoundlanders could compare me. They could compare me with perfection, but that was a comparison in which I could only lose."

10

At Loggerheads and Waterfalls

As the plane flew in narrowing circles, Joey Smallwood watched the great river tumble out of a rocky plateau, crash over a seventy-five-metre precipice, and churn its way toward the Labrador Sea, hundreds of kilometres to the east. He would never forget this first view of Churchill Falls, which had come in 1950, on an idyllic day when the brief northern summer had brightened the tundra with wildflowers. He was enchanted by the sight of one of the natural wonders of the world, but his mind was filled with thoughts of how this vast waterfall, one-and-a-half times as high as Niagara, could be harnessed for power. He was convinced it would make Newfoundland rich.

Two years later, Joey found himself in the Cabinet room of No. 10 Downing Street in London, facing Winston Churchill, once again prime minister after six years in a postwar political wilderness. Joey unrolled a large map — would he ever travel without one? — showing the folds and twists of the raw Labrador countryside. "This is an Empire in itself, sir, and it's British," Joey told him. It needed a great new development company if its wealth was ever to be fully tapped. Something like the Hudson's Bay Company or the East India Company, names that resounded through British history. As Joey talked, the old bulldog behind the desk warmed to the idea. "A great Imperial concept," he pronounced. A few days later, Smallwood took the scheme to a luncheon meeting of British businessmen. They were enthralled by it. The London media were swept up in the excitement. "LABRADOR CALLING BRITAIN," the *Daily Mail* headlined.

Churchill's endorsement was sufficient to gain Smallwood the attention of the House of Rothschild, the great British banking house headed by Antony and Edmund de Rothschild. International investors clamoured to be part of the British Newfoundland Development Corporation (BRINCO), established by an act of the Newfoundland House of Assembly on March 31, 1953. With its charter went rights to 150,000 square kilometres rich in ore, timber, and water power. Rothschild became a major shareholder through the Rio Tinto Co., its international mining giant. Other big investors were Prudential Insurance, Bowater Corporation, Suez Canal Company, Bowring & Company of Newfoundland, the Bank of Montreal, and the Royal Bank of Canada. Smaller shareholders included Winston Churchill and Joey Smallwood himself. The Newfoundland government reserved 9.2 percent of the company's stock for itself. The prospect of profitable power from Churchill Falls glittered in Joey Smallwood's mind for the next twenty years. He had no idea of the struggle he would face or the strife that lay ahead of him before power from Churchill Falls would turn on a single light bulb.*

The promise of a new era of jobs and wealth to flow from Churchill Falls helped spur Smallwood's well-oiled Liberal machine to a third overwhelming victory, in 1956. The margin was thirty-two seats to the Progressive Conservatives' four. The same efficiency could no longer be attributed to the Liberal party in Ottawa. After twenty-two years in power, it was creaking from decay and arrogance. The Louis St. Laurent government found itself embroiled in the great Pipeline Debate, assailed for cutting off debate on an eighty-million-dollar loan to the pipeline's American backers. Voters took their vengeance on June 10, 1957, turning out St. Laurent and handing a minority verdict to his Conservative opponent, the prairie populist John Diefenbaker. Jack Pickersgill held his seat when all but one of Newfoundland's seven ridings stayed Liberal. For the first time since becoming premier, Smallwood had no allies in power in Ottawa. Difficult economic times saw the country struggling with recession, and Newfoundland's need for federal help had never been greater. Politically, matters grew tenser when Diefenbaker engineered a sweep of the country in 1958, winning the largest majority ever. Even so, the count stayed the same in Newfoundland: six-to-one Liberal. In a way, Joey thought, Diefenbaker's victory might be good for Newfoundland. Most of those against Confederation bent naturally to the Conservative side. "The last lingering opposition to Confederation vanished like the wind after Diefenbaker's great victory," he would recall.

---

* Previously known as Hamilton Falls, I have used Churchill Falls throughout, although it was not until 1965 that Joey Smallwood had the name changed to honor Sir Winston, who had died that year.

Despite Joey Smallwood's obsession to develop Churchill Falls, he never forgot the fundamental role forestry played in the island's economy. It was the top creator of jobs and wealth, and determined as he was to build a third great mill, he knew it was the day-to-day logging of eight thousand woods workers that kept forestry atop Newfoundland's economic heap. Unskilled and unorganized — unlike their unionized paper mill brothers who lived in neat company towns — the loggers endured primitive conditions in makeshift work camps of tarpaper shacks, earning $1.05 an hour. The two big companies, Anglo-Newfoundland Development (AND) and the Bowater Company, paid no stumpage fees and virtually no taxes and did no reforestation of the spindly, thinly-treed stands of black spruce under their control.

In 1956 the International Wood Workers of America (IWA) sent a tough forty-something veteran of its British Columbia camps, H. Landon Ladd, to Newfoundland. In six months, he put union cards in the hands of 87 percent of the loggers and applied to the Provincial Labour Relations Board for certification. When the IWA met with the companies, they offered no concessions. The stalemate went to a provincial conciliation board that recommended a wage increase to $1.22 an hour and improvements in camp conditions, including hot and cold water and flush toilets. The IWA accepted the board's findings, but the companies rejected them. Workers voted 98.8 percent to strike, and on January 1, 1959, they put down their saws and stayed in the camps.

Sporadic incidents of violence sparked fears of anarchy in the woods. On February 12, after the RCMP arrested seventy-seven union members following an attack on a camp of strike-breakers, Smallwood stepped into the struggle. He turned to his favourite means of communicating with Newfoundlanders: the radio. The IWA had failed Newfoundland, he told listeners, and the strike had turned into a civil war. He assailed these outsiders for coming "into this decent Christian province and … spreading their black poison of class hatred and bitter, bigoted prejudice."

Coming from a self-professed Socialist and labour union supporter, the speech stunned Joey's union allies; it was clear he was out to break the IWA. Within days, the Newfoundland legislature approved the formation of a new union, the Newfoundland Brotherhood of Wood Workers, and Joey flew to Grand Falls for its inaugural meeting. When the IWA showed no sign of bending, Smallwood sent two more bills to the legislature: one to decertify the IWA and the other to outlaw any union led by men convicted of "such heinous crimes as white slavery, dope-peddling," or other nefarious offences.

The strike might have petered out, lost in the bleak forests of a frozen landscape, but for an event that occurred on the night of March 10, 1959, in the small town of Badger, Newfoundland. Badger had become the stronghold of the IWA, and on that date, several hundred workers rallied on the town's main street. Into their presence strode a detachment of seventy members of the RCMP and the Newfoundland Constabulary. In darkness, the police charged the workers. By the time the melee was over, a twenty-four-year-old member of the Newfoundland Constabulary, William Moss, lay bleeding on the ground. He died the next day in hospital. "CONSTABLES ACCUSED OF BRUTAL ONSLAUGHT," headlined the Toronto *Globe and Mail.*

Smallwood ordered a state funeral for Moss and set up a scholarship in his name. Newfoundland seemed on the edge of anarchy. More RCMP forces would be needed, and the call went to Ottawa for fifty additional officers. "I can't hold off any longer," the Newfoundland head of the force told Leonard Nicholson, the commissioner of the RCMP. After getting the approval of the federal minister of justice, Jamie Fulton, Nicholson ordered a plane to St. John's carrying the extra men. It had no sooner taken off than Fulton phoned to order it back. Prime Minister Diefenbaker, a champion of civil liberties, had vetoed the request. Nicholson, feeling betrayed, resigned. In Parliament a few days later, Diefenbaker would put the blame on Smallwood: "The Premier of Newfoundland has greatly aggravated the present situation in that province by intervening in a labour dispute in a way which apparently goes beyond the usual role of government. The result, as might have been anticipated, has been a violent reaction on the part of the workers."

Diefenbaker was not alone in his criticism. Even Lester Pearson, the Liberal leader, was uncomfortable with Joey's tactics. Jack Pickersgill had to once more come to Joey's aid, negotiating a compromise acceptable to both Smallwood and Pearson: removal of the "heinous crimes" section of the new legislation. In the end, the IWA gave up the strike and advised its members to join Smallwood's Brotherhood of Wood Workers. The new union expired in less than two years, to be replaced by the International Brotherhood of Carpenters. By then, a Royal Commission had confirmed the worst of the charges against the woods camps: "Dark and squalid hovels which would not be used for hen-houses except by the most primitive farmer." The man charged with killing Constable Moss was acquitted when the Crown was unable to produce evidence he had committed the crime.

Joey Smallwood would never offer a definitive explanation of why, as a life-long Socialist and unionist, he took such a strident stand against one of the most reputable and best led of labour unions. In his memoir, *I Chose Canada*, he cites editorials from newspapers across Canada that supported his stand, but concludes obliquely: "It will be a long time before anything more than mere casual violence is used in labour disputes again in Newfoundland."

The controversy helped Smallwood's Liberals win re-election on August 29, 1959, retaining all but one of their thirty-two seats. Victory came even more easily in 1962, with thirty-four Liberals to seven Conservatives and one independent. Both victories were won without much support from labour. A final epitaph to this episode, perhaps the saddest of Joey Smallwood's political life, would come from the pen of Harold Horwood: "The betrayal of the loggers was Joey's one unforgiveable act."

The turmoil of the loggers' strike and Joey Smallwood's ongoing feud with the Diefenbaker government over payments to Newfoundland distracted attention from what was — and was not — happening on the Churchill River. It was just as well. For all the fanfare that heralded the launch of the British Newfoundland Development Corporation, not much had been accomplished in its first ten years. In 1961, with an eye to getting on with hydro development, BRINCO established the Churchill Falls (Labrador) Corporation, with a ninety-nine year lease of water rights. Fanciful schemes were put forward to use the electricity: a smelter to turn Labrador iron ore into steel (who would buy it?); a pulp mill (it could use only a fraction of the power); a plant to make uranium fuel rods using river water for coolant (Britain decided it preferred to make its own). When these wild ideas fell through, it became clear there was only one market that could justify the hundreds of millions of dollars needed to develop Churchill Falls: the great population centres of the U.S. Northeast. Consolidated Edison, the giant New York utility, might be a willing customer. But how to get the power there? There were two options: overland, across the territory of

Quebec; or underwater, buried below the icy waters separating Newfoundland and mainland Canada.

Robert Henry Winters, a Nova Scotia-born engineer who had been a Cabinet minister under Louis St. Laurent, lost his seat in the 1957 election that put John Diefenbaker in office. A handsome, athletic figure of a man, he chose from among many job offers to become chairman of Rio Tinto Mining, the Rothschild company that held shares in BRINCO. The challenge of Churchill Falls proved too great to ignore, and in June 1963 he became its chairman and set out to organize the biggest industrial development in Canadian history — a $1.5-billion project that would produce more than five thousand megawatts of power. It was an undertaking bigger than the building of either the Canadian Pacific Railway or the St. Lawrence Seaway. The arrival of Winters pleased Joey; he was sure that BRINCO would now get on with the job.

Still well-placed politically, Winters drew on his Liberal connections to open discussions with the new premier of Quebec, Jean Lesage, to send Churchill Falls power through two thousand kilometres of high-voltage lines across Quebec. Like many Quebeckers, Lesage resented the fact Labrador had been ceded to Newfoundland, and he was in no mood to accommodate St. John's. He turned out to be a skillful negotiator. A Quebec nationalist, he was piloting his province through a "Quiet Revolution." One of his government's first moves, engineered by his minister of natural resources, René Lévesque, had been to nationalize the province's private power companies. Lesage put Quebec's demands on the table: Nationalize BRINCO and put Churchill Falls under public ownership, administered jointly by Newfoundland and Quebec, with a fifty-fifty division of profit. And for good measure, change the border, use only

Quebec materials and workers, and come up with a better price for Churchill power.

Joey Smallwood got word of Quebec's demands when he was on a trade mission to Sweden in February 1964. He had Robert Winters fly to London, and in a late night meeting in a suite at the Savoy Hotel, Smallwood rejected them all. Joint nationalization, he told Winters, would amount to a partnership between "one elephant, one mouse." There was no doubt who would be the mouse. The old Socialist would have none of it. Betraying BRINCO by buying out its twenty thousand shareholders, he would later write, would have been "vile treachery on Newfoundland's part." The next day in London, Smallwood hired the firm of Preece, Cardew, and Ryder to study the feasibility of laying hydro lines under two turbulent bodies of water: the Strait of Belle Isle between Labrador and Newfoundland, and Cabot Strait, separating Newfoundland and Nova Scotia. There was no doubt it would be a breathtaking task, and an expensive one. Icebergs that came down every spring through the Strait of Belle Isle had a habit of scraping the bottom, putting any underwater cable at risk. The report from the engineers disappointed Joey. An underwater route was possible, but it would cost $350 million dollars more than going overland. Rather than delegate the task of telling the BRINCO board, Joey presented the report himself. The board agreed the task was hopeless.

There was one more alternative: Smallwood struck on the idea of having the Pearson government declare the hydro line in the national interest. That would allow Ottawa to authorize a corridor for BRINCO to build the line through Quebec. Jack Pickersgill saw the insanity of the idea and talked Joey out of it. Smallwood realized a transmission line "through wild, uninhabited wilderness" could be put out of commission any time by "a well-placed bomb here and there." Newfoundland would have to do a deal with Quebec. It would take years of negotiation, and in the end, many Newfoundlanders would see the deal they got as a disaster for their province.

Another three years of negotiations — and a change of government in Quebec — would pass before work would get underway on Churchill Falls. By then, Robert Winters, fed up with the constant haggling — and with the promise of a Cabinet post in the Lester Pearson Liberal government that ousted John Diefenbaker in 1963 — had returned to federal politics. The Lesage government fell on June 6, 1966, just weeks after Hydro-Quebec and BRINCO had reached a tentative agreement. The new premier, Daniel Johnson, even more of a nationalist than Lesage, took his time to consider the deal. Meanwhile, Smallwood had his own election to fight, and on September 8 he won the greatest victory of his career, electing thirty-nine Liberals to three Conservatives. He celebrated by going on an around-the-world trip paid for by Liberal Party supporters. He was in Bangkok when word came on October 7 that the Quebec Cabinet had blessed the deal. Joey summed up his reaction in two words: "Glory hallelujah!"

Between July 1967, when Joey put a silver shovel into a pile of moss to break ground for the first generator, and May 14, 1969, when the final contract was signed, the Churchill Falls (Labrador) Corporation (CFLC) would spend $150 million — all without a firm deal in place. None of that stopped Smallwood from declaring, as he lifted his shovel from the ground, "This is our river, this is our waterfall, this is our land ... We are developing it mainly, chiefly, principally for the benefit of Newfoundland."

Library and Archives Canada, PA-117105

Smallwood with Quebec premier Jean Lesage in Quebec City, April 1964.

The original letter of intent signed by Quebec required that power be flowing within four years — an impossible deadline. The dispute over price and the length of the contract continued right up to the final signing. By the spring of 1969, CFLC was running out of money and Hydro-Quebec knew it; its president sat on the board of Churchill Falls. He was there by virtue of the fact that one of the power companies nationalized by Quebec had held stock in CFLC. With access to all its secrets, Quebec knew what cards to play. At the very last minute, Quebec demanded and got a twenty-five year extension to what had originally been a forty-year agreement. The final contract, running to 2041, called for Quebec to pay three-tenths of a cent per kilowatt hour, with the price dropping to one-fifth of a cent after 2016.

Churchill Falls would not go online until June 1972, when Joey Smallwood was no longer premier of Newfoundland. At the opening ceremony, attended by his successor Frank Moores and Prime Minister Trudeau, he struck the same theme as he had at the groundbreaking ceremony five years before: "This is our land. This is our river. And we will forever make sure ... that it will operate primarily, chiefly and mainly for the benefit of the people of Newfoundland." With that, a button was pushed and a deluge of water poured into giant turbines through a thousand-foot-long underground tunnel. Behind it lay a reservoir the size of Prince Edward Island that would bear the name Lake Smallwood.

The final agreement on Churchill Falls guaranteed Quebec fixed prices, regardless of inflation or the cost of energy worldwide. Within a few years, the Middle East oil crisis would drive up energy prices globally, allowing Quebec to profit hugely by increasing the price of Churchill Falls power sold to the United States. In 2010 Hydro-Quebec would record a net income of $2.5 billion, more than four hundred million dollars of it coming from the resale of Churchill power. In comparison, Newfoundland's net gain has been estimated at twenty million dollars a year.

Newfoundland has twice challenged the Churchill Falls contract in court, and both times it has failed. Every premier since Joey Smallwood has looked for ways to circumvent the pact, without success. The future looks no less bleak: even when the present contract expires, Quebec will remain the only customer for Churchill Falls power, and is unlikely to agree to anything more than a nominal price increase. In 2010, Premier Danny Williams, supported by a federal loan guarantee, announced plans to develop a site downstream on the Churchill River at

Muskrat Falls. The Lower Churchill project would generate only half the power of Churchill Falls, but with the benefit of more advanced technology, it would be exported via underwater cable to Nova Scotia.

Joey Smallwood would never accept responsibility for the Churchill Falls deal, pointing out he never sat at the negotiating table. "The sales contract made with Hydro-Quebec for Churchill Falls power was negotiated and made by the extraordinarily experienced and competent officers of BRINCO and of Churchill Falls Labrador Corporation," he wrote in a letter to the *Evening Telegram*. "No member of my administration ... made the contract for the sale." This is true, but it is also clear that Smallwood was the visionary behind the scheme, and that he kept almost day-to-day control over discussions with Quebec. His diary records constant telephone exchanges with Jack Pickersgill in plotting strategy, as well as his frequent meetings with Premier Lesage, attendance at BRINCO board meetings, and exchanges with every key figure in the project.

As a shareholder in BRINCO, Smallwood was in a conflict of interest by involving himself in Churchill Falls, even if he was not at the negotiating table. More relevant, perhaps, is the question of why he permitted Newfoundland to be bound by a multi-year contract without any provision for inflation. His reaction to the contract, according to BRINCO chairman Donald Gordon, who phoned to give him details, was that Quebec would be getting "pretty cheap power." He was apparently convinced that he had brought Newfoundland a rich bounty in the form of the new town and generating station that was created in Labrador, the twenty-one thousand construction jobs that were filled by Newfoundlanders, and the revenues that would flow to St. John's. He estimated the benefits at six hundred million dollars over the first forty years of the contract. Measured by the economics of the 1960s, this was a lot of money.

Years later, historians would agree that BRINCO, at the edge of bankruptcy and with no prospect of an alternative market or fresh financing, was helpless to resist the demands of Hydro-Quebec. Unconscionable though the demands may have been, they prevailed because their rejection would have meant the end of Joey Smallwood's dream to light the marquees of Broadway with power from Churchill Falls. BRINCO had to go along with Quebec or face an early and embarrassing death. Joey Smallwood had to stand back while BRINCO signed. He consoled himself in the belief that the jobs, royalties, and taxes flowing from Churchill Falls would help to make Newfoundland wealthy.

History produced a different verdict. In 2003 a provincial Royal Commission on the role of Newfoundland in Canada would examine the consequences of a deal in which "huge annual windfall profits go almost entirely to Hydro-Quebec." If even 50 percent of those profits had gone to Newfoundland in the twenty-seven years between 1976 and 2003, it would conclude, the province would have been ahead by eleven billion dollars, and by billions more in the future. In the words of the commission, the fact this was not to be would cast "a long dark shadow" over the place of Newfoundland and Labrador in Canada.

11

Unfinished Business

Joey Smallwood watched with satisfaction as a newly confidant Newfoundland joined with the rest of Canada to celebrate the Centennial of Confederation in 1967 — a Newfoundland that had cast aside its "old benumbing sense of inferiority" in favour of "constant, unending development and advance." The year before, when he had won his greatest ever electoral victory in what he hinted would be his last election, he had brought into his Cabinet a clutch of bright newcomers. They included three young lawyers: John Crosbie, the thirty-six-year-old son of his old mentor and sometimes critic, Ches Crosbie; Alex Hickman, forty-two, a Conservative-minded reformer; and Clyde Wells, not yet turned thirty. Wells remembered, as an eleven-year-old in the tiny railway settlement of Stephenville Crossing, listening to Joey extol the virtues of Confederation from the back of a truck during the 1948 referendum campaigns.

Smallwood had accomplished much of his agenda. Unemployment was still a problem, and the fishery industry was being squeezed by foreign fleets, but Newfoundlanders were more prosperous and the symbols of a modern state were now evident in every town. St. John's, as the capital, boasted a bold new Confederation Building that opened in 1960 to house government offices and the House of Assembly. An expanding Memorial University was rapidly filling a new campus christened by Mrs. Eleanor Roosevelt in 1961. Of all his government's projects, the university was perhaps closest to Joey Smallwood's heart, and he nagged it constantly to add faculties and enlarge community services. It was his dream to make post-secondary education free to Newfoundlanders, and one afternoon in 1965 he went to a student assembly at Memorial to announce the good news. There would be no more tuition, and students were to receive living allowances of up to one hundred dollar a month. They cheered him wildly. It was pure Socialism but it couldn't last. The benefits proved too costly and had to be dropped, although Memorial's fees would remain among the lowest in Canada.

By 1967 another of Joey Smallwood's radical policies, the relocation of residents from isolated outport communities, was entering a new phase. Seven thousand outport occupants, encouraged by grants of a few hundred dollars, had opted to move. Many did so reluctantly, and only after the closing of local schools and nursing stations. A new seven-million-dollar resettlement program, financed heavily with federal money won by Jack Pickersgill, lured another sixteen thousand. Some floated their homes to bigger settlements, others abandoned habitations, gardens, and fishing boats. Families were split, many never found replacement work, and bitterness lingered for years afterwards. Those who moved, however, benefitted from better health care and greater educational opportunities. Lost was the spirit of independence and adventure that from earliest times had fostered a unique slice of Newfoundland life. Showers of abuse have fallen on Joey Smallwood's head over the emptying of the outports, but he always insisted his government had "no policy of centralizing or resettling population." There was help only if "the people themselves wished to move."

St. John's, like other Canadian cities, was becoming accustomed to its own home-grown hippies as the more permissive lifestyle of the 1960s began to take hold. A federal Royal Commission called for the decriminalization of marijuana. Canada's new minister of justice, Pierre Elliot Trudeau, legalized homosexual acts and modernized the divorce law. Joey followed with the creation of local divorce courts and pushed through an amalgamated school board system that reduced control by the churches. When the Liberal party met in Ottawa in April 1968 to choose a replacement to Lester Pearson, it was a toss-up whether Joey would support his friend Robert Winters, whom he admired for his work at BRINCO, or go with Trudeau. He decided on Trudeau and carried three-quarters of the Newfoundland delegates with him. Joey looked forward to Newfoundland voting as enthusiastically for this charismatic new figure as would the rest of the country in the federal election of June 25, 1968. It didn't happen that way. Anti-French sentiment quickly surfaced, and scurrilous pamphlets about Trudeau showed up in people's mailboxes. On top of that, Joey had for the first time lost personal control of naming Liberal candidates, and he faced a revolt in his Cabinet over a scheme to build an oil refinery and chemical complex at Come by Chance. When the votes were counted election night, Progressive Conservatives had upended Smallwood forces by capturing six of the island's seven seats. They carried 53 percent of the vote.

Only Don Jamieson, the broadcaster who with the departure of Jack Pickersgill had become Newfoundland's representative in the Cabinet, survived the Tory deluge. "The Confederation Party died tonight," one old Liberal lamented.

There'd been straws in the wind. In 1967, Conservatives had won two provincial by-elections and in the federal by-election to choose a successor to Pickersgill, Bonavista–Twillingate voters slashed the Liberal majority from 6,400 to just 1,700. Smallwood consoled himself by comparing the reversals to the tide's coming in and going out. The reality was that voters everywhere — except in the smallest outports — had turned against him. The old dreamer was facing voter fatigue. Some of it was the consequence of Pickersgill's departure, but much of it was simply Newfoundland's coming of age. A better educated, more politically sophisticated electorate had tired of their messianic leader. Younger faces were coming into the picture. Ironically, it was Joey Smallwood more than anyone who had built the new society that was now rejecting him.

The Smallwood Cabinet that took office following the 1966 provincial election was probably the strongest and most able since Confederation. Its new members demanded a freer hand in their jurisdictions, and Joey had little choice but to accede to many of their demands. When he presented the latest of his development schemes, a plan for a massive oil refinery put forward by John Shaheen, another Chicago-based promoter, several around the Cabinet table had second thoughts. Shaheen had made his mark in Newfoundland by building the Golden Eagle oil refinery, the province's first, on Conception Bay. Now he had come to Smallwood with a scheme for a much larger refinery at Come by Chance. His plan was to bring in crude oil from the Middle East by supertanker, refine it, and market it on both sides of the Atlantic. The price tag would be $125 million for a refinery that could put out up to six hundred thousand barrels a day. Shaheen had convinced Smallwood to give him an unsecured loan of five million dollars and to guarantee the thirty million dollars worth of bonds he intended to issue.

Bringing John Shaheen to Newfoundland, Smallwood would claim, "was one of my proudest triumphs." His Cabinet didn't always agree. Smallwood named three of his new members — John Crosbie, Clyde Wells, and Alex Hickman — to a committee to review the agreement he had negotiated for Come by Chance. They got some minor concessions, but couldn't budge Shaheen on the government advance. Crosbie and Wells, convinced the economic benefits were too little and the risk too great, resigned from the Cabinet. It was in the middle of the federal election, and their departure to sit as independent Liberals not only marred Smallwood's image of invincibility, but seriously damaged Trudeau's campaign in Newfoundland.

Perhaps the time had come, Joey reflected, to cash in his chips. He told Ed Roberts, his executive assistant, that the people of Newfoundland had spurned him: "It's a personal defeat on a massive scale." The last thing Joey wanted was to be trashed by his own party, as John Diefenbaker had been when the federal PCs turned against "the Chief." Worried about leaving the Liberal Party "dangerously unorganized," Joey decided it was time to go back to the "grass roots." It would take a new organization, and at three meetings in 1968 attended by over three thousand supporters, a new Liberal Association came into being. That fall, the House of Assembly approved the interim financing for John Shaheen's refinery, and Joey sent a letter to the Liberal Association asking for a leadership convention in 1969. It was set for October 31 and November 1, to be attended by seventeen hundred voting delegates.

For years, Joey had made no secret of the fact that when the time came for him to retire, he wanted his close friend and confidant, Dr. Fred Rowe, to replace him. He had moved Rowe from post to post in the Cabinet to give him experience and exposure. Rather than the smooth sailing for Rowe that Joey had expected, a new and threatening opponent emerged from the sidelines: John Crosbie. The announcement of his intention to seek the leadership threw everything into a new light. Rowe, in Joey's opinion, had neither "the grim industry or money" that would fuel Crosbie's campaign, and he saw "no wisdom" in Crosbie becoming premier. The men had been at loggerheads ever since Crosbie had come into the House, and Smallwood was determined to deny him the premiership. At first he tried to have the convention postponed. When the association voted to stick with the scheduled date, Smallwood announced his decision. Resign he would, but he'd also stand for re-election. Rowe agreed to pull out and Joey knew the only other candidate, Alex Hickman, would not be a factor. Joey had unfinished business that needed attention.

Newfoundland had never seen a political campaign like this one. It was the first modern TV-era leadership campaign in the province's history, and it cost a lot of money. Crosbie admits to having spent four hundred thousand dollars and claims Smallwood's expenses must have been over a million dollars, financed largely by contributions from recipients of government contracts. Joey won it on the first ballot: 1,070 votes to 440 for Crosbie. Escorted to the podium by a marching band, Joey gloated at Crosbie's defeat: "All democratic Liberals will accept the choice of the convention. Will Mr. Crosbie come up and make his concession?" Crosbie did so, saying, "I wish him well." Crosbie spent the next two years as part of a Liberal Reform Group before joining the Progressive Conservative Party. By this time, the Tories had a vigorous new leader, Frank Moores. The previous Newfoundland PC leader had resigned after being caught in a police raid on a Montreal brothel.

Back in the House of Assembly after the leadership convention, Joey Smallwood pressed the case for John Shaheen and his Come by Chance refinery. Shaheen's company gave a $150 million contract to a British construction company to build the refinery, convinced the federal government to spend twenty-three million dollars to build a wharf, and signed up to buy one hundred thousand barrels of crude oil per day for the next ten years. It all made jobs for two thousand workers.

By now, Joey Smallwood's revolutionary fervor was running low. He found himself spending time with Richard Nixon, who John Shaheen had hired as his lawyer, on trips to Moscow and other cities. Running his five-year mandate out to the end, he finally called a provincial election for October 28, 1971. This time, Frank Moores and the Progressive Conservatives, strengthened by the addition of John Crosbie and other high profile recruits, were ready. Smallwood's forces were largely the same old line Liberals, with a few notable exceptions. Clyde Wells had resigned his seat to return to his law practice in Corner Brook. Election night brought a deadlock — twenty Liberals, twenty Conservatives, and two independents. All through the winter of 1971–72, the prospect of power shifted back and forth. Behind the scenes bargaining brought what Smallwood would later describe as "the strangest series of maneuverings, twistings, and turnings in our political history." Home from a Florida vacation, he resigned the premiership on January 18, 1972, and recommended that Frank Moores become premier. A hurried Liberal convention in February confirmed Ed Roberts as the new leader. Still, the numbers game was not finished. When the new Moores government met the House of Assembly on March 1, further jockeying left the Liberals in possession of one more seat than the Conservatives. In a twist that has never been fully explained, one Liberal, William Saunders, was absent from the House. Later that day, after the reading of the new government's Speech from the Throne, Moores had Saunders' letter of resignation in his pocket. He asked the lieutenant governor for a new election, and got it. What incentive might have convinced Saunders to resign has never been explained. John Crosbie would hint in his memoirs that money might have changed hands: "If it took $100,000 or more, it was the right move ... Frank [Moores] was good at this kind of stuff." When the election was held on March 24, the Progressive Conservatives won thirty-three seats, the Liberals eight. Joey Smallwood was returned, but the Smallwood era was at an end. Newfoundland, however, had not heard the last of him.

Being out of government came as a shock to Joey Smallwood. He retired to Russwood Ranch and pondered what to do next. His constituents in Placentia East made few demands of him. First on his list was the writing of his memoirs. He'd had dozens of cartons of documents hauled out of the Confederation Building in his last few days in office, giving him everything he needed to write the story of his life. Joey and Clara took long breaks at their condominium in Belleair Bluffs in Florida. There, Joey would pace up and down the living room, thirty paces one way and thirty paces back, up to ten hours a day, dictating his reminiscences. At times, he drove his secretary crazy with typographical instructions, something he'd learned as a printer's devil: "Double space, indent, new paragraph," he'd begin, ending with "full stop, end of paragraph." The result was a six hundred page book, *I Chose Canada: The Memoirs of The Honourable Joseph R. "Joey" Smallwood*. It was published in 1973 by the venerable Macmillan Company and became a national bestseller.

The two great unfinished projects of Smallwood's time in office, Churchill Falls and the Come by Chance oil refinery, both fell into the lap of the Moores government. The Conservatives were unhappy with both of them. When power first began to surge from the penstocks of Churchill Falls, many thought Newfoundland was in for a financial bonanza. With John Crosbie as finance minister, the new Moores government concluded otherwise. It was Crosbie's view that BRINCO should never have been allowed to develop Churchill Falls and that the project should have been a joint venture between Newfoundland and Quebec, as Premier Jean Lesage has urged. The damage could be minimized, Crosbie felt, if the government bought out BRINCO. The negotiations were difficult and the final price for BRINCO's interest in Churchill Falls, $160 million, was much more than Crosbie thought it was worth.

John Shaheen's Come by Chance refinery opened in 1973 in a blaze of publicity. Not one to do things by half measures, Shaheen chartered the *Queen Elizabeth II* at ninety-seven thousand dollars a day to bring celebrities from New York. Joey and Clara flew to New York to join the ocean liner. The timing couldn't have been worse. Within a few months, the world was embroiled in a Middle East oil crisis and the price of oil rocketed from one dollar a barrel to twelve. Shaheen's contract to buy oil from British Petroleum at the world price, originally calculated at a cost of $480 million over ten years, had become a six billion dollar obligation. The refinery lost money every year and would shut down in1976 with debts of five hundred million dollars — including forty-two million owed to the province and forty million to Ottawa. Lawsuits flew back and forth. In 1980, a federal Crown corporation, Petro-Canada, would buy Come by Chance for ten million dollars. Finding it worthless, it would go to a Bermuda company for a dollar before ending up in the hands of North Atlantic Refining, now owned by the Korea National Oil Corp. In 2010 it would be produce 115,000 barrels of oil per day, with exports worth more than two billion dollars a year.

Rumblings of improper dealings between Joey Smallwood, John Doyle, and others involved in various schemes preoccupied the Moores government. John Crosbie thought there was sufficient evidence in several cases to lay charges against Smallwood. At eight o'clock on the morning of December 15, 1972, eight Royal Canadian Mounted Police officers arrived in two cars outside Joey's home at Russwood Ranch. They were joined by eight more officers, plus two who arrived by helicopter, armed with a search warrant to look for incriminating documents. Joey was in Florida, and when his wife Clara answered the door, she let them in and phoned Ramsay Smallwood to come over from his house. The same day, RCMP raided the St. John's apartment of Al Vardy, Smallwood's former deputy minister of economic development. Vardy wasn't there, having decamped for Panama, where John Doyle also resided. Alex Hickman, now minister of justice, said the raids were in connection with "the disposition of funds related to the linerboard mill" Doyle had built in Stephenville. Vardy and Doyle were both charged, with Vardy dying in Miami before he could be brought to trial. No charges were ever laid against Joey Smallwood. It took the RCMP five years to return the files they'd taken from the Russwood Ranch.

Out of office, his memoirs in the bookstores, Joey Smallwood still couldn't resist the call of politics. When Ed Roberts' leadership came up for review in 1974, Joey mounted an unsuccessful challenge against him. Smallwood had admired Roberts ever since he'd hired him as a twenty-four-year-old executive assistant. He'd encouraged him to run for the House of Assembly, and had put him in his Cabinet. Yet by 1975, when it became apparent Frank Moores would soon be calling an election, Smallwood was uncomfortable with Roberts's leadership. Rounding up twenty-seven candidates, he formed the Liberal Reform Party and turned the election of September 16 into a three-way race. He said his intervention marked "the rebirth of Liberalism" but it split the Liberal vote and killed Roberts' chance of victory. Smallwood's candidates ran strongly enough in six ridings to deprive Liberals of victory; without their presence, Ed Roberts would have defeated Moores. The Conservatives were returned with thirty members, to sixteen Liberals and four Reformers, including Joey.

The Smallwood campaign may have had the benefit of Conservative money. Ed Roberts says Craig Dobbins, a confidante of Frank Moores, admitted to him that he raised money for Smallwood. Dobbins was one of Newfoundland's most successful businessmen and would make a fortune running the world's largest helicopter services company. "I don't know if there was a deal between Smallwood and Moores, but Craig told me there was," Roberts says. "Frank was quite capable of it. Craig told me that Moores said, 'If Joe needs help, raise the money.'"

Joey Smallwood sat in the House of Assembly until June 8, 1977. By then, he had returned to the Liberal seats, where Ed Roberts welcomed him back. "I was angry with him, but he was what he was, and anger wasn't going to get me anywhere," Roberts thought at the time. He reminded himself of something Joey had once said to him, "Anger is the least useful of all emotions; its rots you up but it does nothing against the other guy."

Joey's resignation speech was short, something of a rarity for him. He was seventy-seven and no longer had the lungs or the heart to give two-hour orations. "I am now in my twenty-fifth year as a member of this House and for months past, I've wondered why I'm here," he said. "I have no taste for it. I feel I am occupying the seat of someone who would be more useful to my colleagues." Joey was given the expected respectful blessings of his political rivals. Frank Moores lauded his many achievements, adding, "For just about a quarter of a century the people gave to Joe Smallwood their support, their affection, and their trust."

Once freed of the responsibilities of political office, Joey Smallwood took up his favourite pastimes — reading, writing, and world travel. In 1972 he'd gone to Europe to do research for his memoirs, and in London he'd visited the embassy of the People's Republic of China. Wangling a visa, and backed financially with a commission from an unnamed American corporation, he was off to "the other side of the moon." Smallwood saw all the usual sites to which the Chinese took foreign visitors before naively concluding he had seen "more smiling faces, a greater absence of gloominess, a more relaxed look on people's faces" than in any other large country he'd visited. This was at the height of the Cultural Revolution, a decade of death and turmoil of which Joey was apparently unaware. A trip to Cuba, paid for by Fidel Castro, resulted in the remarkable film *Waiting for Fidel*, a wait that proved endless in that he never did see the Cuban leader.

Back in Canada, with tensions rising between French and English, Smallwood threw himself into the national unity debate with speeches across the country extolling the benefits of bilingualism and multiculturalism. But Smallwood's greatest love remained books and writing. With his granddaughter Dale Russell FitzPatrick at his side as his secretary and researcher, a steady stream came from his study, including a picture book called *The Face of Newfoundland* and the political memoirs *The Time Has Come to Tell* and *No Apology from Me*. But it was his cherished *Encyclopedia of Newfoundland and Labrador* that became the great work of his life. He published two volumes before faltering heath and failing finances brought a halt to the project.

On September 24, 1984, while working at Newfoundland House on a third volume, Joey Smallwood suffered a cerebral hemorrhage. He was taken to the Health Sciences Complex at Memorial University, but the stroke had left him unable to write or speak more than a few words. After his return home, daughter Clara became his chief caretaker, shaving and helping him dress and occasionally taking him shopping. He spent a lot of his time reading and when he found an interesting newspaper article, he would tear it out and give it to a family member. He'd expect them to read it and then talk to him about it.

The cost of putting out the first two editions of the encyclopedia had proven a heavy burden to Joey. To raise money, he'd mortgaged the copyright on everything he'd ever written and sold off the most valuable titles of his book collection. The four rarest volumes brought $16,000. A little over a year after his stroke, Joey was sued for $176,161 in unpaid printing bills, and his son William mortgaged his house for $90,000 to settle the claim. Supporters rallied to establish the Joseph R. Smallwood Heritage Foundation. With his granddaughter as manager, it set out to raise $2.5 million to publish three remaining volumes of the encyclopedia and establish the Smallwood Institute of Newfoundland Studies at Memorial University. In the 1970s, Smallwood had deeded Russwood Ranch to the Newfoundland government, on the proviso that he could live there the rest of his life. When Clyde Wells became premier, he put through a bill to return the ranch to Smallwood.*

In one of Joey Smallwood's few remaining public appearances, he went to Government House on December 11, 1986, to be invested a Companion of the Order of Canada. He attended a banquet in his wife's home town, Carbonear, on March 31, 1989, in celebration of the fortieth anniversary of Newfoundland's entry into Confederation. On December 17, 1991, after fighting off several bouts of pneumonia, Joey Smallwood died in his sleep, a week short of his ninety-first birthday. He died as he had lived: a man of good heart, determined to gain his people a better life, ready to use any means to further his aims, oblivious to opposition.

His body lay in state at the Colonial Building, where he had once proclaimed his dream of Confederation. His funeral, on a bitterly cold Saturday at the Catholic Basilica of St. John the Baptist, attracted 1,200 people. The only church in St. John's large enough to accommodate the crowd, it was once, ironically, the bastion of a leader of the anti-Confederate movement, Archbishop Edward Roche. Every politician of note attended the hour-long ecumenical service, including all seven Newfoundland MPs and Prime Minister Brian Mulroney. Joey Smallwood's copper casket, draped with the Newfoundland Union Jack on which rested his Order of Canada, was carried to Mount Pleasant Cemetery. His wife Clara, aged ninety-three, would join him there in 1994.

---

* On Smallwood's death, Russwood Ranch passed to Dale Russell FitzPatrick and Joey's grandson Joseph Smallwood II.

12

The Legend and the Legacy

We love thee, smiling land …
We love thee, frozen land …
We love thee, windswept land …
God guard thee, Newfoundland.
                    — "Ode to Newfoundland"

Joey Smallwood's presence lingers powerfully on in Newfoundland and Labrador, where his life and his legend have been absorbed into a narrative of historic accomplishment and unfulfilled aspirations. Years after his death, the memory of the man burns sharply but his legacy is viewed with mixed feelings, ranging from warmly sentimental to harshly judgmental. Some perceive Joey Smallwood as their savior, the man who rescued his people from an abyss of poverty and despair and began the building of a modern economy. Others see his rush to embrace Confederation and the autocratic rule by which he governed Newfoundland as having deprived its citizens of opportunities and self-respect that were their proper right.

As befits a figure of legendary proportions, Joey Smallwood is one of the very few Canadian politicians immortalized in a work of fiction. Newfoundland author Wayne Johnston, in his novel *The Colony of Unrequited Dreams* — published seven years after Smallwood's death — has Joey guiltily conceding that Confederation was "a terrible but necessary thing." Johnston's Smallwood is a figure of "spindle-thin, emaciated arms and legs," uncomfortable in his first residence as premier, the lavishly furnished Canada House with its "thirty-two rooms, twenty five more than any other house [he] had ever lived in," surrounded by "frauds, shady businessmen, scam artists, shysters, imposters, opportunists," all cadging government grants for "the most unlikely, far-fetched, bizarre schemes for the economic development of Newfoundland, almost all of which flopped or never got off the ground."

Johnston's fictional and often unflattering portrait of Smallwood aroused considerable resentment, although the book became a national bestseller. Johnston had been a nineteen-year-old reporter for the *St. John's Daily News* when he first met Joey in 1977, with Smallwood five years out of the premier's office. Despite this, Smallwood let Johnston know he didn't think much of what he'd been reporting. By the time Johnston finished studying English at Memorial University, he'd decided he wanted to write a big book about Newfoundland, and knew he'd need a big subject. He would finally publish *The Colony of Unrequited Dreams* in 1998 to join a cascade of books by a new generation of Newfoundland writers.

A commemorative bust of Joey Smallwood on display at the University Centre at Memorial University of Newfoundland.

Johnston had grown up in St. John's among a people rich in culture who could, according to a later Premier, Danny Williams, "easily have lost it all" without Smallwood's intervention. It was Smallwood, the Conservative Williams acknowledged at a ceremony in 2008, whose "vision for this province and its people played a significant role in preserving and developing our culture." Williams reminded his listeners that Smallwood had started Newfoundland's network of arts and cultural centres, was the driving force behind the establishment of Memorial University, had instituted an Arts and Letters Award, established a film company, and had himself written or edited twenty-one books.

"Premier Smallwood's memorial can be found in the astonishing productivity of Newfoundland's artists on paper, on canvas, on film, in song and play and novel, and in sculpture, painting and photography," Williams said. "Almost sixty years after joining the Canadian federation, we still have a unique culture to celebrate and to share with the world."

Joey Smallwood's presumed shortcomings — his heavy-handed control of Cabinet and legislators, his questionable economic development schemes, and even his benign corruption — make easy pickings for critics. Rarely recognized, and of more enduring significance, were his ground-breaking investments in education and his ardent support of the arts that created the environment that would produce Johnston and others of his generation.*

Among his harshest critics were his political opponents. John Crosbie has written that Smallwood "was more than a despot. He was corrupt ... he not only betrayed the trust and

---

* Even the shortest list of Newfoundland artists reveals astonishing variety: writers Michael Crummy, Wayne Johnston, Lisa Moore, Michael Winter, Kathleen Winter, Bernice Morgan, E.J. Pratt, Gwyn Dyer; painters David Blackwood, Christopher Pratt, Helen Parsons Shepherd; actors and TV performers Seamus O'Regan, Gordon Pinsent, Rick Mercer, Mary Walsh, Linden MacIntyre, Rex Murphy, Ray Guy; and musical groups Wonderful Grand Band and Great Big Sea.

stole the dreams of our poor province, but also stole their money, living like a colonial King Tut." The first New Democrat elected provincially in St. John's, Gene Long, maintained that "despite a modest few achievements and no end of bragging rights about them, Smallwood went on to become a great embarrassment and a terrible liability to Newfoundland."

Twenty years after Joey Smallwood's death, an astonishing reversal of economic fortune has occurred in Newfoundland. After enduring Canada's highest unemployment, lowest per capita income, fastest declining population, highest taxes, and weakest financial position, Newfoundland suddenly found itself an engine of economic growth. It had become a "have" instead of a "have not" province, recording surpluses while other provinces run deficits, contributing to rather than receiving equalization grants, and showing strong gains in employment. An energy powerhouse fuelled by offshore oil development and forthcoming hydropower projects, strengthened by an emerging high-tech and knowledge economy, Newfoundland's future seems assured, at least in the short-term. Yet within this picture of presumed affluence can be found seeds of discontent.

The Royal Commission that examined Newfoundland's position in Confederation in 2003 concluded: "The overwhelming sentiment is against separation and in favour of improving our place in Canada." Only 12 percent of Newfoundlanders favoured becoming an independent country, the commission said. But it also criticized the status quo:

> Since Confederation, its hydroelectric resources in Labrador have been developed for the benefit of Quebec; its oil resources have been developed in a manner that makes Canada

the primary beneficiary; its fishery has all but disappeared under the stewardship of the federal government; double-digit unemployment has persisted for the last 15 years, and in the last decade 12 per cent of its population has been lost to out-migration.

Despite these laments, the Royal Commission's balance sheet declared Newfoundland a net beneficiary of Confederation, receiving two billion dollars a year more than Ottawa drew from the province in revenue. These figures have since come into balance. Since the commission's report, the legacy of Churchill Falls has been cleansed to some degree by plans for the Muskrat Falls project on the Lower Churchill River that would export power via underwater cable, with the potential of greatly profiting Newfoundland. Production from four offshore oil fields on the fringe of the Grand Banks will exceed one hundred million barrels a year, growing exponentially until the inevitable decline sets in, probably around 2030. Newfoundlanders have always "gone away" to work, but the ten thousand or more employed in the Alberta oil sands have transferred one hundred million dollars a year of income back home, fuelling buying and building booms in many communities. Visitors to St. John's should not be surprised that the Edmonton station of Global Television is one of the city's more widely watched cable channels.

Before the global economic crisis of 2008, advocates of Newfoundland's independence often cited Ireland and Iceland as island countries that had prospered on their own, each fulfilling Joey Smallwood's famous oxymoron of a "great small nation." The economies of those countries crashed when their banks, unfettered by strict financial regulations of the type prevailing in Canada, gave out billions of dollars in risky loans. Would an independent Newfoundland have fallen prey to the same temptation? Would an independent Newfoundland have husbanded its natural resources more carefully than Canada or would it, like Joey Smallwood's government, have poured public money into subsidies for private companies whose factory ships destroyed in a decade a fishery that had flourished for centuries? Would Newfoundland on its own have been able to attract foreign investment from around the world? Would it have been able to pull itself up by its own bootstraps and reach a living standard approximating that which it enjoys as a Canadian province? The answers are unknowable and can be only guessed at. Based on available evidence, the verdict on Joey Smallwood's life and tenure must be that he led Newfoundland to a vastly better future within Confederation than it could have found outside it.

Also unknowable is the province's future. How will Newfoundland and Labrador deal with the eventual exhaustion of its oil, the uncertainties of exporting power, its heavy reliance on the public sector for jobs, the disappearance of rural communities, and the decline of its working age population? (The province has the highest median age in Canada.) "What do you do," I was asked, "when there's nobody left to shovel the snow?"

Many Newfoundlanders who have come of age since the death of Joey Smallwood see him as a figure of the distant past, even a slightly ridiculous character, a big spender, a different kind of politician than is acceptable in Newfoundland today. But they cannot dismiss his positive impact on their homeland.

Edward Roberts worked more closely with Joey Smallwood than perhaps any other person. He recalls asking Smallwood what had been the most important change in Newfoundland since Confederation. His answer: "The children. After Confederation, you never again saw a child with no clothes — no children wearing rubber boots with no socks or clothes made out of sacks."

Former Premier Clyde Wells, notwithstanding disagreements, considers Smallwood to have made a greater contribution to the welfare and future of the people of Newfoundland than any person in the province's history. In his funeral eulogy, Wells called Smallwood's greatest monument an unseen one: "Our status as equal citizens of the most favoured nation on earth."

On an earlier occasion, another premier, Frank Moores, invoked a more romantic image of Joey Smallwood when he characterized him as "one of those rare individuals whose fires burn with the steady incandescence of a fixed and constant star." That star, for all its flawed brilliance, is certain to shine undimmed for a very long time to come.

Postscript

Buried in the vaults of Library and Archives Canada (LAC), secret documents compiled by the Royal Canadian Mounted Police detail the force's inquiry into certain activities of Joseph R. Smallwood and others associated with him during and after the period he served as premier of Newfoundland and Labrador. The files rest in the "restricted material vault" of the LAC warehouse in Gatineau, Quebec. Our freedom of information application for access to these files succeeded in obtaining copies of only about thirty pages (out of probably hundreds), with most of them highly censored and none revealing either the full scope or the precise nature of the RCMP's activities. There were additional files, but we will never know what was in them, as they have been destroyed without being microfilmed. Did they contain records of RCMP spying? A reasonable assumption, in view of the admission by the Canadian Security Intelligence Service (CSIS)

that RCMP surveillance reports on former prime ministers John Diefenbaker and Lester Pearson were destroyed in the 1980s.

The Newfoundland premier had a long and conflicted history with the RCMP. He declined to allow RCMP policing in the province, maintaining the Royal Newfoundland Constabulary as the province's civil police force. He sought RCMP assistance in combating the loggers' strike of 1959 and would have had it but for Prime Minister Diefenbaker's refusal to allow the dispatch of the requested fifty additional officers. And after leaving office, Smallwood became the object of RCMP criminal investigation in December 1972.

Joey Smallwood was not the first Canadian premier to have been subject to RCMP surveillance. The political activities of Tommy Douglas, premier of Saskatchewan and later leader of the New Democratic party, were monitored by the RCMP and later the Canadian Security Intelligence Service (CSIS) from as early as the 1930s, when he was a Baptist church minister. Files on Douglas released in 2005 reveal the full nature of the scrutiny. Did the self-avowed socialist Smallwood receive the same kind of treatment? We do not know. The retention at LAC of the greater part of the Smallwood files prevents us from rendering a historical judgment on the part of either the police or the politician.

The Access to Information Act allows the government to withhold information that relates to the government of a foreign state, that might be injurious to the conduct of international affairs or the defence of Canada, that is shielded by solicitor-client privilege, or that qualifies as personal information.

This covers a lot of territory. One of Canada's leading researchers into aging, Dr. Bertrand Desjardins, told me that Canada has "a warped view of protection of privacy" so extreme that it is impossible to accurately determine the exact nature of the aging of the Canadian population. Documents relating to historic occurrences from the Second World War are still under lock and key at LAC. In one example, information on the Canadian government's 1943 banning of a half-dozen social, political, and religious organizations — none were ever demonstrated to have been a threat to Canada's ability to wage war — is still restricted.

Back to the Smallwood files. From examining the few pages concerning the activities of promoter John Doyle that did not come totally obliterated (as in the case of the letters passing from the RCMP's legal services division to the criminal prosecutions section of the Department of Justice), we learn that Mounties dispatched officers to Europe to investigate an alleged Smallwood bank account that Doyle was said to have transferred $750,000 to as a reward for "friends in Newfoundland."

An inquiry conducted by the Restrictive Trade Practices Commission (RTPC) into wrong doing in the affairs of Doyle's company, Canadian Javelin, failed to find evidence that any such payment was ever made. Smallwood refused to appear before the commission and later sued its six members, claiming to have been wrongly accused of corrupt business dealings with Doyle. He also complained to the RCMP about the manner in which it had transmitted information about him to Frederick Sparling, director of the corporate affairs branch of the RTPC, whose investigation led to the seizure of Doyle's shares in Canadian Javelin and ultimately the end of the company.

The accusations against Smallwood originated in a letter from an undisclosed informant to the RCMP (the name is blacked out in a report to RCMP commissioner R.H. Simmonds) concerning the supposed Smallwood bank account and a mysterious Liechtenstein corporation, Societe Transhipping. An RCMP memorandum of January 31, 1984, advised that "the

Force has now completed its review of the complaint lodged by Mr. Smallwood and find no basis for criticism of the action of any of our members." This was a not-unexpected conclusion of an internal investigation. The files that were released are equally bereft of any information on RCMP activities in regard to the raid on Mr. Smallwood's home on December 15, 1972.

The propensity of government officials to withhold access to historic information is regrettable on just about every count imaginable. It denies Canadians of a fuller understanding of their heritage, casts what may be unwarranted suspicion on the actions of bodies such as the Royal Canadian Mounted Police, and may leave the reputation of otherwise entirely admirable personalities such as Joey Smallwood under a cloud of calumny and doubt. Canadians deserve better.

Chronology of Joey Smallwood

Joey and His Times

1900
December 24. Joseph "Joey" Roberts Smallwood born in outport of Gambo, Newfoundland.

1910
September. Joey enters boys' boarding school of Bishop Feild College when his father's brother, Fred Smallwood, agrees to finance his education. He leaves the college in 1916 after a quarrel.

1918
October. Joey Smallwood secures a job as a reporter at St. John's *Evening Telegram*.

Canada and the World

1900
The federal government increases the head tax on Chinese immigrants.

1910
Amid great controversy, the Laurier government brings the Royal Canadian Navy into existence.

1918
November 11. Armistice brings the First World War to an end.

Joey and His Times

1920
October. Smallwood arrives in New York after working on newspapers in Halifax and Boston. He secures a reporting job on the *New York Evening Call*, a Socialist newspaper.

1923
May. Smallwood meets and courts Lillian Zahn, daughter of Jewish refugees from Galicia, but the relationship ends when her mother realizes he is not Jewish.

Joey Smallwood spurns his position at the *New York Times* to work for film producer Ernest Shipman, raising funds for films to be made in Newfoundland and Prince Edward Island; he returns to New York.

1925
February. Leaving New York for good, Smallwood becomes an organizer in Newfoundland for the International Brotherhood of Pulp, Sulphite, and Paper Mill Workers.

August. He organizes the Newfoundland Railway track workers, and by yearend wins them a revocation of their pay cut.

November 23. Smallwood marries Clara Oates of Carbonear, niece of his boarding house owner. He starts the weekly newspaper *Labour Outlook*.

1926
February. Smallwood becomes an editor of St. John's daily *Globe*.

Canada and the World

1920
The Group of Seven's first exhibit opens in Toronto, establishing an independent genre of Canadian art.

1923
The Chinese Immigration Act of 1923 bans most Chinese from entering Canada, with special exceptions made for certain classes of immigrants.

1925
Arthur Meighen's Conservatives win the most seats in the federal election, but Mackenzie King's Liberals form a minority government with the assistance of the Progressives.

1926
The United Farmers of Canada, a federal party, is formed by a merger

Joey and His Times	*Canada and the World*
	of the Saskatchewan Grain Growers Association and the Farmers' Union of Canada.
	In the "King-Byng" affair, Mackenzie King assails the action of Governor General Lord Byng in denying King dissolution of Parliament; the Meighen government is quickly defeated and King wins the subsequent election.
1927	**1927**
March 1. During a visit by Smallwood to London, Britain's Privy Council confirms Newfoundland's ownership of Labrador. On his return to Newfoundland, Smallwood launches the *Humber Herald*.	Canadian author Mazo de la Roche publishes *Jalna*, the first in a sixteen-part series.
1929	**1929**
November 18. Twenty-eight people in Burin Peninsula die from a tidal wave after a 7.2 earthquake off Grand Banks.	October 29. On this day, known as Black Tuesday, the U.S. stock market suddenly collapsed, heralding the beginning of the Great Depression.
1930	**1930**
Smallwood launches a new St. John's weekly, the *Watchdog*, owned by Prime Minister Sir Richard Squires.	February. Cairine Reay Mackay Wilson becomes Canada's first female senator.
1932	**1932**
June. Smallwood runs as a Liberal for the Newfoundland House of Assembly and is defeated, along with the Squires government.	November 26. James Edward Hervey MacDonald, member of the Group of Seven, dies.
1937	**1937**
Smallwood publishes his *Book of Newfoundland* and begins work as	Trans-Canada Air Lines, predecessor to Air Canada, is formed. A second

Joey and His Times

columnist for St. John's *Daily News*, writing "From the Masthead" under byline of "The Barrelman." He also begins a nightly broadcast as "The Barrelman" on VONF, which runs for over six years.

1939

Smallwood buys a forty-acre tract on Kenmount Road, St. John's, and launches a chicken farm, which fails due to a shortage of feed stock. He later experiments with raising hogs, and after the United States establishes an air base at Gander, he sets up a pig farm to supply pork to servicemen.

1945

December 11. During a stopover in Montreal, Smallwood reads of Britain's plan to allow Newfoundlanders to decide their future form of government.

1946

June 21. After publishing a series of letters in St. John's *Daily News* in support of Confederation, Smallwood is elected as the delegate to the National Convention for Bonavista Centre, with the largest majority in Newfoundland.

November 5. The National Convention votes 25–18 to defeat Smallwood's resolution to send a delegation to Ottawa to discuss terms of union with Canada.

Canada and the World

public agency, the Canadian Broadcasting Commission, becomes the CBC, launching a national radio service in Canada.

1939

September 10. Canada declares war on Germany, entering the Second World War. In order to demonstrate Canada's independence, the declaration has been delayed to a week after Britain's entry into the war.

1945

August 15. Japan surrenders following the dropping of atomic bombs on Hiroshima and Nagasaki, and the Second World War is at an end.

1946

June 25. Roméo Dallaire, the Canadian senator and general known for his peacekeeping work in Rwanda, is born.

Joey and His Times

1948

January 29. By a vote of 29–16, the National Convention defeats Smallwood's motion to have "Confederation with Canada" placed on a referendum ballot along with the options "return to Responsible government" and "retention of Commission government."

March 10. After public protest and petitions, the British government rules Confederation to be included in referendum.

June 3. Responsible government places first and Confederation second in the referendum; Commission government is third and is dropped.

July 22. Confederation wins referendum over Responsible government, 78,323 to 71,334.

1949

March 31. Newfoundland joins Confederation.

April 1. Joey Smallwood sworn in as premier of Newfoundland

May 27. The first Newfoundland provincial election yields a Liberal majority: twenty-two Liberals, five Conservatives, and one independent.

June 27. Federal election: Newfoundland elects five Liberals and two Conservatives.

Canada and the World

1948

November 15. Louis St. Laurent becomes the 12th prime minister of Canada, succeeding Mackenzie King, who has been the country's longest serving Prime Minister.

1949

April 4. Canada joins the North Atlantic Treaty Organization (NATO).

Joey and His Times

1950
March. Joey Smallwood engages Alfred
Valdmanis as his economics advisor.

1951
June. Newfoundland and Labrador
Corporation (NALCO) is formed
as a Crown corporation and given
exploration and development rights
in Labrador.

November 26. Provincial election:
twenty-three Liberals, five
Conservatives.

1952
August. Eager for new industry,
Joey Smallwood goes to London,
England, with an idea for a massive
development company and enlists the
support of Prime Minister Winston
Churchill and Rothermere interests.

1953
January 31. Joey Smallwood
recruits Jack Pickersgill, clerk of the
Canadian Privy Council, to stand as
a Liberal MP in Newfoundland.

March 31. The British
Newfoundland Corporation
(BRINCO) is established.

August 10. Federal election: Liberals
win all seven Newfoundland seats.

September. John C. Doyle's Canadian
Javelin Ltd. agrees to buy NALCO, but
the deal falls through when Javelin
shares are delisted by the Toronto and
Montreal stock exchanges.

Canada and the World

1950
Canada is called to action in the
Korean War.

1951
September 1. Nellie McClung,
noted Canadian feminist and social
activist, dies.

1952
Elizabeth II becomes Queen of the
United Kingdom and the British
Empire.

1953
The National Library of Canada is
created.

Joey and His Times	*Canada and the World*
1954	**1954**
February 7. Joey Smallwood fires his economics advisor, Alfred Valdmanis.	Hurricane Hazel kills eighty-one people, most of them in Toronto.
March. Smallwood grants John Doyle mineral rights to 2,400 square miles in Labrador; a survey proves up two billion tons of iron ore are in the Wabush Lake area.	
April 24. Alfred Valdmanis is arrested by RCMP in New Brunswick on charges of extortion and bribery.	
September 16. Alfred Valdmanis is found guilty on two charges of accepting $470,000 in bribes from German companies; he is sentenced to four years.	
1956	**1956**
October 2. Provincial election: thirty-two Liberals, four Conservatives.	Lester B. Pearson devises a diplomatic resolution to the Suez Crisis, later winning the Nobel Peace Prize.
1957	**1957**
May 12. Ramsay Smallwood, son of Joey, is severely injured in a helicopter crash that kills Ramsay's wife	John Diefenbaker's Progressive Conservatives form a minority government, bringing to an end a twenty-two-year-long Liberal government.
June 10. Federal election: six Liberals, one Conservative elected in Newfoundland.	
1958	**1958**
March 31. A repeat of the last federal election: six Liberals and one Conservative elected in Newfoundland.	The Progressive Conservatives receive a majority mandate.

Joey and His Times

1959

February 12. Joey Smallwood announces the formation of a new loggers' union to replace the striking International Woodworkers of America (IWA); the later decertification of IWA results in the Badger riot, in which a member of the Newfoundland Constabulary is killed. The Federal government's refusal to send RCMP reinforcements causes the resignation of RCMP commissioner Leonard Nicholson.

March. Bitter public fight begins between Joey Smallwood and Prime Minister John Diefenbaker over Term 29 of the Confederation agreement.

August 29. Provincial election: thirty-one Liberals, three Conservatives, two United Newfoundland Party.

1962

June 18. Federal election: six Liberals and one Conservative returned.

November 19: Provincial election: thirty-four Liberals, seven Conservatives, and one independent.

1963

April 8. Federal election: Liberals win all seven Newfoundland seats. The Liberal Lester B. Pearson replaces John Diefenbaker as prime minister.

Canada and the World

1959

February 20. The Avro Arrow project is cancelled amidst controversy; Prime Minister Diefenbaker cites budgetary reasons.

1962

The Cuban Missile Crisis strains international relations with the threat of nuclear war.

1963

When Prime Minister Diefenbaker opposes the American plan of installing Bomarc missiles on Canadian soil to defend against potential Soviet attacks, his government collapses and an election is called.

Joey and His Times

1964
January. The first federal-provincial fisheries conference is held in Ottawa.

May. Joey Smallwood opposes the Maple Leaf flag, and finally agrees on the Union Jack as Newfoundland's provincial flag.

June 23. Negotiations with Quebec on the Churchill Falls hydro deal collapse when Hydro-Quebec's offer falls short of BRINCO's asking price.

July 20. Joey Smallwood officiates at the opening of John Doyle's Wabush Iron mine; Doyle is convicted of securities violations in the United States and jumps bail rather than serve his three-month term.

1965
November 8. Federal election: all seven Newfoundland seats won by Liberals.

1966
September 8. Provincial election: thirty-nine Liberals, three Conservatives.

October 7. Hydro-Quebec signs a letter of intent to buy Churchill Falls power, insisting on delivery starting within four years.

1967
September 18. Jack Pickersgill resigns as federal minister of transport and MP and then becomes chairman of the Canadian Transportation Commission.

Canada and the World

1964
Social insurance numbers are issued to Canadians for the first time.

1965
Trans-Canada Airlines becomes Air Canada.

1966
May 18. Canadian Paul Joseph Chartier dies in an attempt to detonate a bomb in the House of Commons.

1967
This is the year of the Canadian Centennial, and a year-long celebration is held, including Expo '67 in Montreal.

Joey and His Times	*Canada and the World*

July 17. Construction begins on the Churchill Falls power project.

October. William Smallwood, son of Joey, is involved in a custody battle and loses his Liberal nomination.

1968
June 25. Federal election: Conservatives win six seats, Liberals one, following Pierre Trudeau's replacement of Lester B. Pearson as prime minister with a majority mandate.

1968
Pierre Elliott Trudeau replaces Lester Pearson and calls a general election for June 25. Amidst a wave of "Trudeumania," a Liberal party majority government is elected.

May. Two Smallwood Cabinet ministers, John Crosbie and Clyde Wells, resign over Smallwood's scheme to finance John Shaheen's Come by Chance oil refinery.

1969
May 14. An agreement is finalized with Hydro-Quebec on the Churchill Falls power project; a sixty-five-year agreement sets the price of three mills per kilowatt hour (three-tenths of a cent), dropping to two mills (one-fifth of a cent) by 2016.

1969
The Front de libération du Québec (FLQ), a terrorist organization, bombs the Montreal Stock Exchange.

November 1. In a leadership convention called by Joey Smallwood, he defeats his main challenger, John Crosbie, 1,070 votes to 440.

1971
October 28. Provincial election: twenty-one Conservatives, twenty Liberals, one New Labrador Party.

1971
When accused of mouthing swear words at the opposition, Pierre Elliott Trudeau replies that the words were actually "fuddle duddle."

Joey and His Times

December 6. The first two generating units of Churchill Falls begin delivery of electricity to Hydro-Quebec.

1972
January 18. Joey Smallwood resigns as premier of Newfoundland after recounts confirm a Conservative victory; Frank Moores becomes premier.

March. The Moores government finds John Doyle's Canadian Javelin in default on loans for construction of the Stephenville linerboard mill and takes over the company after $122 million invested by Smallwood government.

June 16. The Churchill Falls Hydro project is officially opened by Prime Minister Trudeau and Premier Moores, in the presence of Joey Smallwood.

October 30. Federal election: four Liberals and three Conservatives elected in Newfoundland.

As private citizen, Joey Smallwood tours China at the height of the Cultural Revolution and later praised it as a country of "no unemployment, no inflation, no crime, no prostitution, no drug addiction, no alcoholism," adding, "what a land!"

March 24. Provincial election: thirty-three Conservatives, eight Liberals, one New Labrador Party.

Canada and the World

1972
Canada bans cigarette advertisements in film, radio, and television.

Joey and His Times

Canada and the World

1973
In his autobiography, *I Chose Canada*, Joey Smallwood concludes, "I have lived many lives, and they have been exciting, every one."

April. Joey's son-in-law Edward J. Russell, husband of Clara, dies of a self-inflicted gunshot wound at Russwood Ranch.

December. John C. Doyle is arrested on four hundred counts of fraud over the Stephenville linerboard project; he is released on $75,000 bail and promptly flees to Panama, where he dies in 2000 at age eighty-five, a fugitive from justice.

1974
July 8. Federal election: Newfoundland elects four Liberals and three Conservatives,

1975
Provincial election: thirty Conservatives, sixteen Liberals, one independent Liberal, plus four Joey Smallwood Liberal Reform candidates; he is elected in Twillingate.

1977
June 8. Joey Smallwood resigns from the House of Assembly.

1979
May 22. Federal election: Four Liberals, two Conservatives, and the first New Democrat elected in

1973
The *Royal Canadian Air Farce* begins as a radio program.

1974
The Official Language Act establishes French as Quebec's only official language, though the legality of the act is disputed by some and later updated.

1975
The construction of the CN Tower, or Canadian National Tower, is completed, though the structure will not open to the public until 1976.

1977
As part of the Silver Jubilee of Elizabeth II, the queen tours Canada.

1979
May 29. Mary Pickford, the storied Canadian actress, also known as "America's Sweetheart," passes away.

Joey and His Times

Newfoundland. Joe Clark becomes
prime minister as a Conservative
minority government replaces the
administration of Pierre Trudeau.

1980
February 18. Federal election:
Pierre Trudeau and the Liberals are
returned to power; Newfoundland
chooses five Liberals and two
Conservatives.

1984
Volume one of Joey Smallwood's
*Encyclopedia of Newfoundland and
Labrador* is published, followed by
volume two in 1984. Three more
volumes are published by 1994 by
the Joseph R. Smallwood Heritage
Foundation.

February 29. Prime Minister Pierre
Trudeau announces his retirement.

September 4. Federal election:
Newfoundland seats split four
Conservatives and three Liberals;
Prime Minister Mulroney and the
Progressive Conservative Party

Canada and the World

1980
April 12. Terry Fox begins his
Marathon of Hope across Canada to
raise money for cancer research.

1982
Queen Elizabeth proclaims the
Constitution Act in an Ottawa
ceremony, replacing British North
America Act as Canada's constitution.
The Constitution Act includes the
Charter of Rights and Freedoms.
The refusal of Quebec government
to assent to the Constitution Act
creates political strain that is not yet
completely overcome.

1984
September 3. Thomas Bernard Clark
Brigham allegedly plants a bomb
in Central Station in Montreal,
which kills three French tourists and
injures dozens more.
Pierre Trudeau resigns. He is
succeeded by John Turner who
serves briefly before the Progressive
Conservative party under Brian
Mulroney is elected with the largest
ever parliamentary majority.

Joey and His Times

replaces the Liberal government of John Turner.

September 24. Joey Smallwood suffers a cerebral hemorrhage.

1986
December 11. Joey Smallwood invested as a companion of the Order of Canada.

1988
November 21. Federal election: the Conservative Party is re-elected in the "free trade" election; Newfoundland elects five Liberals and two Conservatives.

1989
March 31. Joey Smallwood attends a dinner in Carbonear celebrating the 40th anniversary of Newfoundland's entry into Confederation.

1991
December 17. Joey Smallwood dies, one week before his 91st birthday.

Canada and the World

1986
Speakers for the House of Commons are selected by secret ballot from this year forward.

1988
Prime Minister Brian Mulroney issues an official apology for the internment of Japanese Canadians during the Second World War, following the 1941 attack on Pearl Harbor. The Mulroney government is re-elected.

1989
Despite opposition from those with concerns about what it would mean for Canada's sovereignty, social programs, and other trade agreements, Canada enters the Free Trade Agreement with the United States.

1991
The Gulf War begins with Operation Desert Storm to drive Iraqi forces out of Kuwait. The Iraqi Army is destroyed, but the U.S.-led forces leave Saddam Hussein in power.

Bibliography

BOOKS

Bassler, Gerald P. *Alfred Valdmanis and the Politics of Survival*. Toronto: University of Toronto Press, 2000.

Blake, Raymond B. *Canadians at Last: Canada Integrates Newfoundland as a Province*. Toronto: University of Toronto Press, 1994.

Callahan, William R. *Joseph R. Smallwood: Journalist, Premier, Newfoundland Patriot*. St. John's: Black Tower, 2003.

Clark, Rex, ed. *Contrary Winds: Essays on Newfoundland Society*, St. John's: 1986.

Crosbie, John C. *No Holds Barred: My Life in Politics*. Toronto: McClelland & Stewart, 1997.

Encyclopedia of Newfoundland and Labrador, Vols. I–V. St. John's: Newfoundland Book Publishers Limited and Harry Croft Publications Ltd., 1981–1995.

Goulding, Jay. *The Last Outport, Newfoundland in Crisis*. Toronto: 1982.

Guy, Ray, *The Smallwood Years*. Portugal Cove: Boulder Publishing, 2008.

Gwyn, Richard. *Smallwood: the Unlikely Revolutionary*. Toronto: McClelland & Stewart, 1968.

Horwood, Harold. *Joey: The Life and Political Times of Joey Smallwood*. Toronto: Stoddart, 1989.

Jamieson, Don. *No Place for Fools, The Political Memoirs of Don Jamieson*. St. John's: 1989.

Johnston, Wayne. *The Colony of Unrequited Dreams*. Toronto: Knopf, 1998.

Long, Joe. *Suspended State: Newfoundland Before Canada*. St. John's: Breakwater Books, 1999.

Major, Kevin, *As Near to Heaven by Sea*. Toronto: Penguin Canada, 2001.

Mowat, Farley. *The New-Founde-Land*. Toronto: McClelland and Stewart, 1989.

O'Flaherty, Patrick. *Leaving the Past Behind: Newfoundland History from 1934*. St. John's: Long Beach Press, 2011.

Pottle, Herbert L. *Newfoundland: Dawn Without Light: Politics, Power, People in the Smallwood Era*. St. John's: 1979.

Prowse, D.W. *A History of Newfoundland, from the English, Colonial and Foreign Records*. London : Eyre and Spottiswoode, 1896.

Rose, Alex. *Who Killed the Grand Banks?* Toronto: John Wiley & Sons Canada, 2008.

Rowe, Frederick. *The Smallwood Era*. Toronto: McGraw Hill-Ryerson, 1985.

Smallwood, Joseph R. *I Chose Canada: The Memoirs of the Hon. J.R. 'Joey' Smallwood*. Toronto: Macmillan of Canada, 1973.

_____. *No Apology from Me*, St. John's: 1979

_____. *The Best of the Barrelman*, St. John's: 1998

_____. *The Time Has Come to Tell*, St. John's: 1979

_____, ed. *The Book of Newfoundland*, 4 vols., St. John's: 1967

_____, ed. *Encyclopedia of Newfoundland and Labrador*, 3 vols., St. John's:1935

Smallwood, Reginald. *My Brother Joe: Growing Up With the Hon. Joseph R. ("Joey") Smallwood*. St. John's: Privately published, 1995.

Thoms, James R., ed. *Call Me Joey*. St. John's: Harry Cuff Publications, 1999.

Thomson, Dale C. *Louis St. Laurent: Canadian*. Toronto: Macmillan of Canada, 1967

Vance, Jonathan. *Unlikely Soldiers: How Two Canadians Fought the Secret War Against Nazi Occupation*. Toronto: HarperCollins, 2008.

Walsh, Bren. *More Than a Poor Majority: The Story of Newfoundland's Confederation With Canada*. St. John's: 1985

Wells, Janice. *Frank Moores: The Time of His Life*. Toronto: Key Porter, 2008.

WEBSITES

A comprehensive history of Newfoundland and Labrador can be found at *www.heritage.nf.ca/law/default.html*. The Centre for Newfoundland Studies of Memorial University has links to a range of web sites at *www.library.mun.ca/qeii/cns/links.php*.

VIDEOS

Waiting for Fidel. www.nfb.ca/film/waiting_for_fidel.
Little Fellow From Gambo. www.nfb.ca/film/little_fellow_from_gambo_joey_smallwood.

Index